The Way of the Fathers

The Christian life is the true Jacob's ladder on which the angels ascend and descend. Meanwhile, the Lord stands above, holding out His hand to those who slip, sustaining by His vision the weary steps of those who ascend.

—St. Jerome

The Way of the Fathers

of the

Praying with the Early Christians

Mike Aquilina

Our Sunday Visitor Publishing Division
Our Sunday Visitor, Inc.
200 Noll Plaza
Huntington, Indiana 46750

The citations of the works of the Fathers in this book are taken from a variety of sources, including the works of the Venerable John Henry Newman and the Edinburgh series of the Fathers. The author has revised the language for the modern reader. If any copyrighted materials have been inadvertently used without proper credit being given in one manner or another, please notify Our Sunday Visitor in writing so that future editions may be corrected accordingly.

Our Sunday Visitor Publishing Division
Our Sunday Visitor, Inc.
200 Noll Plaza
Huntington, IN 46750

ISBN: 087973-334-9
LCCCN: 99-75028

The cover design is based on the sixth-century illustration by Abbot Johannes Klimax used as an instruction to monks. Good monks climb steadily heavenwards, toward perfection, while bad monks are dragged to Hell by black devils. The illustration became an icon in the twelfth century and is at St. Catherine Monastery, Mount Sinai, Sinai Desert, Egypt. Used with permission; Eric Lessing/Art Resource, NY.

Cover design by Tyler Ottinger
Edited by Lisa Grote
PRINTED IN THE UNITED STATES OF AMERICA
334

For Father Frederick Cain

Pastor and hometown patrologist
who keeps the church unlocked and generously shares
his library of the Fathers.

Table of Contents

The Way of the Fathers

Foreword

So you feel the desire to pray.

Jesus was very clear about how one should approach personal prayer: "Whenever you pray, go into your room and shut the door and pray to your Father who is in secret, and your Father who sees in secret will reward you. . . . Do not heap up empty phrases as the gentiles do. . . . Your Father knows what you need before you ask Him" (Mt 6:6,7a, 8b).

Yet even as we pray privately, we do not pray autonomously. We pray in and with the Church in a communion that extends beyond the present moment, reaching back in time over the ages. Our prayer is at one with the prayers of men and women of every age who have lifted their hands, voices, and hearts to God and have sought His second coming in glory — men and women who have striven to remain interiorly, spiritually, awake and vigilant, but also Christ-like in outward conduct. Wonderfully for us, some have left windows into their experience, revealed very often in homilies, discourses, or pastoral and even personal letters. Foremost among our forebears are those men whom the Church has called her "Fathers."

These men, closer in time to the Lord's own lifetime — living in a time when memories of Him and the apostolic age were fresh and pristine — are essentially the "founding fathers" of Christianity. They picked up where the Apostles left off and continued the development and refinement of theological reflection and doctrinal formulation. The Church received from them the very framework of her organization, necessary to effective evangelization of the world, in keeping with the Lord's commission. The Fathers were men who had a unique capability of living eschatologically, which is to say, of perceiving one continuing moment of prayer and doxology leading humankind and indeed the whole cosmos to its definitive salvation in Christ.

Sure guides are of great help to us. For prayer is vital for our life in Christ. In reading the Fathers of the Church, you will discover a wellspring of spirituality that is Trinitarian, dogmatically orthodox, and thoroughly permeated with the mind of the Church as expressed in her liturgy. Frequently, the Fathers are narrowly appealed to, only for purposes of doctrinal clarification. This is unfortunate, for the men with whom you are about to become better acquainted were always primarily concerned with how Christians might most fruitfully pursue the habit of prayer, developing with the aid of grace an ever deeper contemplation of the mysteries of our being "in Christ" and always emanating from the liturgy of the whole Church.

These were men of diverse occupations. Some were bishops — even married bishops; others were simple monks, hut-dwellers, songwriters, artists, and fathers of families. A few even lived the strange (for us) existence of dwelling atop pillars. Today, these men are known to us as saints. But they also came from the very stuff of lives much like our own. We are bound to them by a love for the Church, which, after all, is people living in their own time, seeking to live forever with the Father, the Son, and the Holy Spirit. The Fathers' struggles, humor, piercing intellect, and wisdom could take hold of your own hand, heart, and mind and lead you into true prayer. Might you be willing to trust them?

If you wish to become an ever more willing disciple of Christ, steadier in the habit of prayer and firmer of faith, then allow yourself to listen to what the Fathers have to say to you. You can be sure that they are eager to act as your guides and mentors. They will become, if you are open to them, your spirit-filled fathers in the Lord. They are willing to share with you the substance of their mystical vision, their most intimate experience, their most thoughtful advice. They have never let us down; nor have we exhausted their inestimable riches.

It is very often said that ours is an age in which people seek instant gratification. The Fathers will have no part in this. Instead, they will lead you slowly, gently, almost cautiously along. This is because there can be no real progress without a stripping off of the old man, after we have confronted his reality in us. In order to "put on Christ," as the baptismal liturgy says, we must first undergo a complete change, a *metanoia* involving our attitudes toward people, situations, things, ourselves, and even the Church. As you probably already know, you will have to be very honest with yourself in order to achieve this. The Fathers will have something to work with in you only if you are prepared to be as honest with yourself as they had to be with themselves.

Here is the genius of this little book compiled by Mike Aquilina. This is no commentary. He lets the Fathers speak for themselves. They will make their own what are your everyday concerns and will help you place them under the protection of God's saving power. Here are addressed such topics as suffering, anxiety, grace, the world, the heart, marriage and family, integrity, the body, and death. These men of the Church will beckon you more deeply into her incomparable inner life. Walk along with them. Converse with them as you go. They are sure companions along The Way that alone leads us to the kingdom of Heaven, "from glory to glory."

— The Rt. Rev. Archimandrite Joseph (Lee)

Abbot, Monastery of the Holy Cross, Washington, D.C.; Academic Dean, St. Josaphat Ukrainian Catholic Seminary; and Instructor in Patristics, Dominican House of Studies

Preface

Like all good parents, the Fathers of the Church taught their children to pray. By their words and their lives, the ancient Christian teachers led their supernatural family — sometimes gently, but always firmly — in the ways of the spirit.

We should count ourselves among their children. For, with Christ ever present, the Church knows no generations. We are always living in the first hearing of the Gospel; and we are always living in the end times. We are, even today, children of illustrious Fathers.

The Fathers of the Church are a select group of early Christian teachers. The Church has long revered them and given them a privileged place of doctrinal authority. Yet their authority extends beyond doctrine and theology, to the depths and heights of the interior life. They were, above all, masters of prayer. Indeed, the Fathers would never have tolerated the strict academic separations made by contemporary Church professionals; to the Fathers, Scripture, spirituality, and theology did not demand three distinct and unrelated courses of study. The Fathers' unity of life is summed up neatly in this maxim: A theologian is one who prays, and one who prays is a theologian.

This book is for those who pray and for those who want to pray. I want to pray, and that is how this book came to be. While writing another volume, *The Fathers of the Church: An Introduction to the First Christian Teachers*, I kept a copybook of passages I found especially intriguing, inspiring, or puzzling. I intended to keep these aside for further consideration in prayer. The collection grew, until my editor-in-chief, Greg Erlandson, suggested that I make it a book all its own.

The result is *The Way of the Fathers* — a somewhat deceptive title, I admit. The selections do not add up to a comprehensive "spirituality of the Fathers." No such book could be written, because the Fathers were a wildly diverse lot. I selected, instead, readings that would be most applicable for my contemporaries who are living in the ordinary circumstances of modern work, family, culture, and leisure. Thus, I have given minimal attention to certain key concerns of the Fathers. Monasticism, for example, is hardly mentioned here, though the subject occupies many volumes by the men I have quoted.

The quotations are arranged loosely according to themes, beginning with matters most familiar to us, such as creation and human nature, then proceeding to God and the sacraments before examining the life of prayer and growth in virtue. The book ends with a consideration of the last things in life.

I am pleased to share these one thousand small treasures from our common family heritage. All the selections in this book come from the age of the Fathers — the period stretching from the middle of the first century to the middle of the eighth — though not every quotation is from a Father. I have also included passages from early Church councils, anonymous documents, and the works of minor Christian writers.

Most of these excerpts were drawn from nineteenth-century British works on the Fathers, especially the works of Venerable John Henry Newman and the multi-volume Edinburgh series of the Fathers. I have taken the liberty of revising the language to suit a twenty-first-century readership. Those who wish to study the Fathers' spirituality in greater depth should take up Johannes Quasten's masterful four-volume study, *Patrology*.

Please begin, though, as the Fathers began every endeavor. Begin with prayer. Pray with this book. Take each of our Fathers' words and refer them to Jesus. Ask that you might acquire the mind of Christ, which was both the desire and the hallmark of the Fathers of the Church. Slowly, in silence, make these thoughts your own.

As you pray, I ask you also to pray for me.

—Mike Aquilina

The Way of the Fathers

Creation

1 All nature is good.

—St. Augustine

2 The very harmony of creation, its preservation and governing, teach us that there is a God Who has put all this together and keeps it together.

—St. John of Damascus

3 The orderly arrangement of the whole universe is a kind of musical harmony whose maker and artist is God.

—St. Gregory of Nyssa

4 The sun and moon, with the companies of the stars, roll on in harmony according to His command, within their prescribed limits, and without any deviation. The fruitful earth, according to His will, brings forth food in abundance, at the proper seasons. . . . The ocean, impassable to man, and the worlds beyond it, are regulated by the same enactments of the Lord. . . . All these the great Creator and Lord of all has appointed to exist in peace and harmony. He does good to all, but most abundantly to us who have fled for refuge to His compassion through Jesus Christ.

—Pope St. Clement I of Rome

5 Heaven and earth and all that is in the universe cry out to me from all directions that I, O God, must love You, and they do not cease to cry out to all so that they have no excuse.

—St. Augustine

6 There is no one so uncivilized, and of such a crude disposition, that, raising his eyes to heaven, he does not understand from the very magnitude of the objects, from their motion, arrangement, constancy, usefulness, beauty, and temperament, that there is some providence — though he does not know by what god's providence all the visible universe is governed.

—Lactantius

7 It is possible to see Him who has made all things in wisdom by way of inference through the wisdom that appears in the universe.

—St. Gregory of Nyssa

8 When we look at the order of creation, we form in our mind an image, not of the essence, but of the wisdom of Him who has made all things wisely.

—St. Gregory of Nyssa

9 It is the same with all things that raise the mind to transcendent goodness, all these we can call apprehensions of God, since each one of these sublime meditations places God within our sight. For power, purity, constancy, freedom from contrariety — all these engrave on the soul the impress of a divine and transcendent mind.

—St. Gregory of Nyssa

10 Even in small things, the same spirit is revealed. We admire the Creator, not only as the framer of heaven and earth, of sun and ocean, of elephants, camels, horses, oxen, leopards, bears, and lions, but also as the maker of tiny creatures, ants, gnats, flies, worms, and the like.

—St. Jerome

11 The mind determined to ignore bodily things will find itself weakened and frustrated. Since the creation of the world, the invisible things of God are clearly seen by way of images. We see images in the creation which, although they are only dim lights, still remind us of God. For instance, when we speak of the holy and eternal Trinity, we use the images of the sun, light, and burning rays; or a running fountain; or an overflowing river; or the mind, speech, and spirit within us; or a rose tree, a flower, and a sweet fragrance.

—St. John of Damascus

Human Nature

12 Know, O beautiful soul, that you are the image of God. Know that you are the glory of God. Know, then, O man, your greatness, and be vigilant.

—St. Ambrose of Milan

13 God imprinted on your nature the likeness of the glories of His own nature, as if molding the form of a carving into wax.

—St. Gregory of Nyssa

14 In the nature that is to enjoy God, there must be something kindred to Him who is to be partaken of.

—St. Gregory of Nyssa

15 Knowing, then, the nobility we share, and how we are seedlings from heaven, let us do nothing that would put our nature to shame.

—Nemesius of Emesa

16 You have created us for Yourself, and our hearts are restless till they rest in You.

—St. Augustine

17 Our evil comes from our lack of resemblance to God and our ignorance of Him. On the other hand, our great good consists in our resemblance to Him.

—St. Methodius of Olympus

18 There is a God-shaped hole in every man that only Christ can fill.

—St. Augustine

19 O soul, only He who created you can satisfy you. If you ask for anything else, it is your misfortune.

—St. Augustine

20 When we consider these facts about man, how can we exaggerate the dignity of his place in creation? In his own person, man joins mortal creatures with the immortal?

—Nemesius of Emesa

21 Whoever knows the feebleness of human nature has acquired an experience of the strength of God.

—St. Maximus the Confessor

22 Sick, we truly stand in need of our Savior; having wandered, of one to guide us; blind, of one to lead us to light; thirsty, of the fountain of life of which whosoever partakes shall no longer thirst; dead, we need life.

—St. Clement of Alexandria

23 God willed this to be the nature of man: that he should eagerly desire two things: religion and wisdom.

—Lactantius

24 The chief good of man is in religion only; for the other things, even those that are supposed to be peculiar to man, are found in the other animals, too.

—Lactantius

25 The term *happy* cannot belong to him who lacks what he loves, whatever it may be; or to him who has what he loves, if it is hurtful; or to him who does not love what he has, although it is good in perfection. For one who seeks what he cannot have suffers torture; and one who has what is not desirable is cheated; and one who does not seek what is worth seeking is diseased.

—St. Augustine

26 What then am I, O my God? What is my nature? A varied and multiform life of powerful immensity.

—St. Augustine

27 I do not succeed in comprehending all that I am.

—St. Augustine

28 When you hear that the divine majesty is exalted above the heavens, that its glory is inexpressible, its beauty ineffable, and its nature inaccessible, do not despair of ever beholding what you desire. It is within your reach; you have within yourselves the standard by which to apprehend the divine. For He who made you did at the same time endow your nature with this wonderful quality.

—St. Gregory of Nyssa

29 Let us consider, brethren, of what material we were formed, who we are, and with what nature we came into the world, and how He Who formed and created us brought us into His world from the darkness of a grave, and prepared His benefits for us before we were born. Therefore, since we have everything from Him, we ought in everything to give Him thanks.

—Pope St. Clement I of Rome

The Search

30 To know oneself has always been the greatest of all lessons. For, if anyone knows himself, he will know God. And, in knowing God, he will become like Him.

—St. Clement of Alexandria

31 Let it be your first care not to deceive yourself.

—St. Melito of Sardis

32 Within me was a hunger of that inward food, Yourself, my God.

—St. Augustine

33 I bore about a shattered and bleeding soul, weary of being borne by me, yet finding nowhere to rest.

—St. Augustine

34 In groaning and tears alone I found a little refreshment.

—St. Augustine

35 I will take my stand where my parents placed me as a child, until the clear truth be found out.

—St. Augustine

36 Let everything perish! Dismiss these empty vanities! And let us take up the one search for truth.

—St. Augustine

37 I desire to know God and the soul. Nothing else? Nothing.

—St. Augustine

38 Much time had I spent in vanity, and had wasted nearly all my youth acquiring the sort of wisdom made foolish by God. Then once, like a man roused from deep sleep, I turned my eyes to the marvelous light of the truth of the Gospel, and I perceived the uselessness of "the wisdom . . . of the rulers of this world, who are doomed to pass away" (1 Cor 2:6). I wept many tears over my miserable life and I prayed that I might receive guidance to admit me to the doctrines of true religion.

—St. Basil the Great

39 I will not hesitate to search if I find myself in doubt; I will not be ashamed to learn if I find myself in error. . . . Let him continue along with me, whoever with me is certain; let him search with me, whoever shares my doubts; let him turn to me, whoever acknowledges his own error; let him rebuke me, whoever perceives my own.

—St. Augustine

40 If I am mistaken, that means that I exist.

—St. Augustine

41 What I feared to part with was now a joy to surrender.

—St. Augustine

42 Pray that, above all things, the gates of light may be opened to you; for these things cannot be perceived or understood by all, but only by the man to whom God and His Christ have imparted wisdom.

—St. Justin Martyr

Sacred Scripture

43 Love Holy Scripture and wisdom will love you. Love her, and she will keep you. Honor her, and she will embrace you.

—St. Jerome

44 Reading Scripture is like reading letters from the other world.

—St. Augustine

45 To be ignorant of the Scripture is not to know Christ.

—St. Jerome

46 Holy Scripture is sufficient for teaching. Yet it is good to exhort one another in the faith and refresh one another with our discourses.

—St. Anthony of Egypt

47 A man who is well grounded in the testimonies of Scripture is the bulwark of the Church.

—St. Jerome

48 The Bible is a stream wherein the elephant may swim and the lamb may wade.

—Pope St. Gregory the Great

49 Apply yourself diligently to the reading of the Sacred Scripture. Apply yourself, I say. For we who read the things of God need much application, lest we should say or think anything too rashly about them.

—Origen

50 There is nothing empty and nothing idle in divine literature, but what is said is always said for some useful purpose.

—Cassiodorus

51 A monk who wanted to acquire a knowledge of the Scriptures ought not to spend his labor on the works of commentators, but rather to keep all the efforts of his mind and intentions of his heart set on purifying himself from carnal vices. For when these are driven out, at once the eyes of the heart, as if the veil of the passions were removed, will begin as it were naturally to gaze on the mysteries of Scripture.

—St. John Cassian

52 The Old Testament proclaimed the Father clearly, but the Son more darkly. The New Testament plainly revealed the Son, but only indicated the deity of the Spirit. Now the Holy Spirit lives among us and makes the manifestation of Himself more certain to us.

—St. Gregory Nazianzen

53 Sing the Psalms of David; and diligently study the Gospel, which is the completion of the other.

—Anonymous (*Teaching of the Twelve Apostles*)

54 The contents of Scripture are the outward forms of certain mysteries and the images of divine things.

—Origen

55 When you find in Holy Scripture anything you did not believe before, believe it without doubt.

—St. Augustine

56 We are not allowed to affirm what we please. We make Holy Scripture the rule and the measure of every tenet. We approve of that alone which may be made to harmonize with the intention of those writings.

—St. Gregory of Nyssa

57 If you believe what you like in the Gospel and reject what you do not like, it is not the Gospel you believe, but yourself.

—St. Augustine

58 We meet to read the books of God, if anything in the nature of the times bids us look to the future or open our eyes to the facts. In any case, with those holy words we feed our faith, we lift up our hope, we confirm our confidence.

—Tertullian

59 The study of inspired Scripture is the chief way of finding our duty. For in it we find both instruction about conduct and the lives of blessed men delivered in writing, as some breathing images of godly living, for the imitation of their good works.

—St. Basil the Great

60 When those who follow heresies venture to avail themselves of the prophetic Scriptures, in the first place they will not make use of all the Scriptures, and then they will not quote them entire, nor as the body and texture of prophecy prescribe. But selecting ambiguous expressions, they wrest them to their own opinions, gathering a few expressions here and there, not looking to the sense, but making use in the mere words.

—St. Clement of Alexandria

61 All men do not understand Scripture in the same sense, but diverse men diversely, this man and that man, this way and that way, expound and interpret its sayings. . . . Therefore it is necessary, in order to avoid these great windings and turnings of errors so various, that the line of expounding the prophets and Apostles be directed and drawn according to the rule of the sense of the Catholic Church.

—St. Vincent of Lerins

62 The exegesis of the divine oracles demands a soul cleansed and spotless; it demands also a keen intelligence, which can penetrate into the things of God and venture into the shrine of the Spirit. It needs, moreover, a tongue that can serve that intelligence and worthily interpret what it understands.

—Theodoret of Cyrrhus

63 You who are accustomed to take part in the divine mysteries know, when you receive the Body of the Lord, how you protect it with all caution and veneration lest any small part fall from it, lest anything of the consecrated gift be lost. For you believe, and correctly, that you are answerable if anything falls from there by neglect. But if you are so careful to preserve His Body, and rightly so, how do you think that there is less guilt to have neglected God's Word than to have neglected His Body?

—Origen

Tradition

64 We all need, with one accord, to follow the guidelines of our holy Fathers, doing nothing in contention, but, unanimous in every aim of good devotion, to obey, the Lord helping us, the divine and apostolic constitutions.

—Pope St. Gregory the Great

65 You and I share the same teachers of God's mysteries and spiritual fathers, who from the beginning were the founders of your Church.

—St. Basil the Great

66 We hold communion with the apostolic churches because our doctrine is in no respect different from theirs. This is our witness of truth.

—Tertullian

67 If I were to destroy what those who came before me established, I should be justly convicted of being not a builder but an overthrower.

—Pope St. Gregory the Great

68 The Apostles were sent as Fathers; to replace those Apostles, sons were born to you who were constituted bishops. . . . The Church calls them Fathers, she who gave birth to them, who placed them in the sees of their Fathers. . . . Such is the Catholic Church. She has given birth to sons who, through all the earth, continue the work of her first Fathers.

—St. Augustine

69 We ought to remain in the Church that was founded by the Apostles and continues to this day. If ever you hear of any that are called Christians taking their name not from the Lord Jesus Christ, but from some other, for instance, Marcionites, Valentinians . . . you may be sure that you have not the Church of Christ there, but the synagogue of Antichrist. For the fact that they took rise after the foundation of the Church is proof that they are those whose coming the Apostle foretold. And let them not flatter themselves if they think they have scriptural authority for their assertions, since the devil himself quoted Scripture, and the essence of the Scriptures is not the letter, but the meaning. Otherwise, if we follow the letter, we too can concoct a new dogma and assert that such persons as wear shoes and have two coats must not be received into the Church.

—St. Jerome

70 If you have any care for me, remember me as a father.
—St. Anthony of Egypt

71 Farewell, and love us as a child, for we love you as a father.
—St. Ambrose of Milan

Church

72 The world is a sea, in which the Church is set, like a ship tossed in the deep, but not destroyed. For she has with her the skilled Pilot, Christ.

—Hippolytus of Rome

73 If we continue to love one another and to join in praising the Most Holy Trinity — all of us who are sons of God and form one family in Christ — we will be faithful to the deepest vocation of the Church.

—St. Polycarp of Smyrna

74 The sacrifice of the Church is the word breathing as incense from holy souls, the sacrifice and the whole mind being at the same time unveiled to God.

—St. Clement of Alexandria

75 One who seeks the Church seeks Christ.

—St. Ambrose of Milan

76 Who says that the great Church is only a small part of the earth? The great Church is the whole world.

—St. Augustine

77 Only the Catholic Church is the Body of Christ. . . . Outside this body, no one is animated by the Holy Spirit.

—St. Augustine

78 There is no salvation outside the Church.

—St. Cyprian of Carthage

79 He can no longer have God for his Father, who has not the Church for his mother.

—St. Cyprian of Carthage

80 O wondrous mystery! One is the Father of all, one also the Word of all, and the Holy Spirit is one and the same everywhere. And there is only one Virgin Mother; I love to call her the Church.

—St. Clement of Alexandria

81 She is one mother, plentiful in fruitfulness. From her womb we are born, by her milk we are nourished, by her spirit we are animated.

—St. Cyprian of Carthage

82 Where the Church is, there also is the Spirit of God; and where the Spirit of God is, there is the Church, and all grace. And the Spirit is truth.

—St. Irenaeus

83 The Church is a faithful and ever watchful guardian of the dogmas that have been entrusted to her charge. In this sacred deposit, she changes nothing, she takes nothing away, she adds nothing to it.

—St. Vincent of Lerins

84 This is the holy Church, the one Church, the true Church, the Catholic Church, which fights against all errors. She may be attacked, but cannot be overcome. The gates of hell shall not prevail against her.

—St. Augustine

85 The one and only Catholic and Apostolic Church can never be destroyed, though all the world should seek to make war against it. It is victorious over every impious revolt of the heretics who rise up against it.

—St. Alexander of Alexandria

86 As there are many rays of the sun, but one light . . . thus also the Church, shone over with the light of the Lord, sheds forth her rays over the whole world, yet it is one light that is everywhere diffused.

—St. Cyprian of Carthage

87 Hear this, you of the laity, the elect Church of God. The people were formerly called "the people of God," and "a holy nation." You, therefore, are the holy and sacred Church of God, enrolled in heaven, a royal priesthood, a holy nation, a chosen people, a bride adorned for the Lord God, a great Church, a faithful Church.

—Anonymous (*Teaching of the Twelve Apostles*)

88 We are a body knit together as such by a common religious profession, by unity of discipline, and by the bond of a common hope.

—Tertullian

89 The Church herself, which should be the appeaser of God in all things, what is she but the exasperater of God?

—Salvian

90 Remember, Lord, Your Church. Deliver it from all evil and perfect it in Your love; and gather it together from the four winds — the Church that has been sanctified — into Your kingdom which You have prepared for it.

—Anonymous (*Teaching of the Twelve Apostles*)

91 Feed us, the children, as sheep. Yes, Master, fill us with righteousness. Pasture Your own. Feed us, O Tutor, on Your holy mountain, the Church, which towers aloft, which is above the clouds, which touches heaven.

—St. Clement of Alexandria

92 Follow the custom of the Church where you happen to be.

—St. Ambrose of Milan

93 Let us choose to belong to the Church of life, that we may be saved. I do not think you are ignorant that the living Church is the Body of Christ.

—Pseudo-Clement

God

94 Though our lips can only stammer, still we chant the greatness of God.

—Pope St. Gregory the Great

95 We worship one God in Trinity and Trinity in Unity.

—Athanasian Creed

96 This Trinity is one God from Whom, through Whom, and in Whom all things exist.

—St. Augustine

97 Never was the Son wanting to the Father, nor the Spirit to the Son; but without variation and without change, the same Trinity abides forever.

—St. Gregory the Wonderworker

98 There certainly was not a time when God was not the Father.

—Dionysius of Alexandria

99 The Father is always the Father. He is the Father, since the Son is always with Him, on account of Whom He is called the Father.

—St. Alexander of Alexandria

100 God fulfilled the office of a true father. He Himself formed the body; He Himself infused the breath of the soul. Whatever we are, it is altogether His work.

—Lactantius

101 We speak not as supplying His name; but for want we use good names, in order that the mind may have these as points of support, so as not to err in other respects. For each one by itself does not express God; but all together are indicative of the power of the Omnipotent.

—St. Clement of Alexandria

102 The God of the Christians is not confined by place, but being unseen fills heaven and earth, and is worshiped and glorified by the faithful everywhere.

—Anonymous (*Martyrdom of Justin*)

103 He, indeed, is of an unchangeable nature, perfect in every way and lacking nothing. . . . For what progress can the wisdom of God make? What increase can truth itself and God the Word receive? In what respect can the life and the true light be made better?

—St. Alexander of Alexandria

104 No one can rightly express Him wholly. For, on account of His greatness, He is ranked as the All and is the Father of the Universe.

—St. Clement of Alexandria

105 The divine nature, whatever it may be in itself, surpasses every mental concept.

—St. Gregory of Nyssa

106 On the threshold of the knowledge of God, one does not seek to know His essence. No human being could arrive at it. No one knows it but God. But, if you can, ponder deeply His attributes — His eternity, His infinity, His invisibility, His goodness, His wisdom, His power that creates, governs, and judges creatures. For he best merits the name of theologian who seeks to discover, however little, the truth of His attributes.

—St. Maximus the Confessor

107 We can know what God is not, but we cannot know what He is.

—St. Augustine

108 The preeminent excellence of divinity transcends human speech.

—St. Augustine

109 In what concerns God, the thought is truer than the word, and the reality is truer than the thought.

—St. Augustine

110 The Godhead is purity, freedom from passion, and separation from all evil. If these are in you, then God is in you.

—St. Gregory of Nyssa

111 O God, Who are always the same, let me know myself and know You.

—St. Augustine

112 Late have I loved You, Beauty so ancient and so new! Late have I loved You. You were within me, but I was outside myself, and there I searched for You.

—St. Augustine

113 God loves each of us as if there were only one of us.

—St. Augustine

114 Come to the Father.

—St. Ignatius of Antioch

Jesus Christ

115 Who is He? Briefly learn: the Word of truth, the Word of incorruption that generates man by bringing him back to the truth — the goad that urges us to salvation — He Who expels destruction and pursues death — He Who builds up the temple of God in men that He may cause God to take up His abode in men.

—St. Clement of Alexandria

116 He is the door of the greatest temple. He is the way of light. He is the guide to salvation. He is the gate of life.

—Lactantius

117 The Son of God became the Son of Man so that sons of men could become sons of God.

—St. Athanasius

118 The omnipotent God engaged in combat with His most bitter enemy, not in the strength of His own majesty, but in our human infirmity.

—Pope St. Leo the Great

119 Christ saved men not with thunder and lightning, but as a wailing babe in the manger and as a silent sufferer upon the Cross.

—St. Jerome

120 His compassion for us compelled Him — Who cannot be compelled — to be born in a human body at Bethlehem.

—St. Methodius of Olympus

121 The Word of God, Jesus Christ, because of His great love for mankind, became what we are in order to make us what He is Himself.

—St. Irenaeus

122 He was made man that we might be made God, and He manifested Himself by a body that we might receive the idea of the unseen Father; and He endured the insolence of men that we might inherit immortality.

—St. Athanasius

123 The Word was not impaired in receiving a body, that He should seek to receive a grace, but rather He deified that which He put on, and more than that, gave it graciously to the race of man.

—St. Athanasius

124 By partaking of Him, we partake of the Father; because the Word is the Father's own.

—St. Athanasius

125 Unless He were true God, He could bring us no help; and if He were not true man, He could offer us no example.

—Pope St. Leo the Great

126 He has become man, so that He might deify us in Himself! And He has been born of a woman, and begotten of a virgin, in order to transfer to Himself our erring generation, and that we may become ever more a holy race, and "partakers of the divine nature," as St. Peter wrote (2 Pet 1:4).

—St. Athanasius

127 Born as a son and led forth as a lamb, sacrificed as a sheep, buried as a man, He rose from the dead as God, being by nature both God and man.

—St. Melito of Sardis

128 We call Him Helper and Savior, the power of whose name even the demons fear, and today, when they are exorcized in the name of Jesus Christ, crucified under Pontius Pilate, Governor of Judea, they are overcome.

—St. Justin Martyr

129 What new mystery is this? The Judge is judged, and holds His peace; the Invisible One is seen, and is not ashamed; the Incomprehensible is laid hold upon, and is not indignant; the Illimitable is circumscribed, and does not resist; the Impossible suffers, yet does not avenge; the Immortal dies, and answers not a word; the Celestial is laid in the grave, and endures!

—St. Melito of Sardis

130 The very tomb of His slain body, small and narrow though it be, is more revered than the countless palaces of kings, more honored than the kings themselves.

—St. John Chrysostom

131 Look for Him who is above time — the Timeless, the Invisible, who for our sake became visible.

—St. Ignatius of Antioch

132 We do not yet see Christ made "all things in all," as the Apostle says; still we can find Him bit by bit in all.

—St. John Cassian

133 Christ prays for us, prays in us, is prayed to by us. He prays for us as our Priest; He prays in us as our Head, is prayed to by us as our God. We therefore recognize our voice in Him and His in us.

—St. Augustine

The Holy Spirit

134 It is impossible for anyone to acquire the grace of God if he does not have the Holy Spirit, in Whom . . . all the gifts of God consist.

—Didymus the Blind

135 The Holy Spirit is the plenitude of all gifts, and nothing is given in the Divinity without Him, because all the advantages that are received from the favor of God's gifts flow from this Fountainhead.

—Didymus the Blind

136 He is called Spirit, as "God is Spirit" (Jn 4:24), and "the breath of our nostrils, the Lord's anointed" (Lam 4:20). He is called Holy, as the Father is Holy, and the Son is Holy; for, to the creature, holiness was brought in from outside, but to the Spirit holiness is the fulfillment of nature, and it is for this reason that He is described not as being sanctified, but as sanctifying.

—St. Basil the Great

137 There is close relationship with God through the Spirit, for "God has sent the Spirit of His Son into our hearts, crying, 'Abba! Father!' " (Gal 4:6).

—St. Basil the Great

138 What then is the Paraclete's administrative office but this: the direction of discipline, the revelation of the Scriptures, the reform of the intellect, the advancement toward the better things?

—Tertullian

139 One possesses the Holy Spirit to the extent he loves the Church of Christ.

—St. Augustine

140 He founded His Church upon the rivers, making it, through His divine legislation, capable of receiving the Holy Spirit, from Whom, as from their Fountainhead, the different graces flow as fountains of living water.

—Didymus the Blind

141 What the soul is to the body of man, the Holy Spirit is in the Body of Christ, which is the Church.

—St. Augustine

142 The Spirit of God is direct, authoritative, the fountain of wisdom, life, and holiness.

—St. John of Damascus

143 Come, Holy Ghost, Who, ever one,
Reignest with Father and with Son,
It is the hour, our souls possess
With Thy full flood of holiness.

—St. Ambrose of Milan

The Triumph of the Cross

144 They hanged upon a tree Him Who stretches out the earth; they transfixed Him with nails Who laid firm the foundation of the world; they circumscribed Him Who circumscribed the heavens; they bound Him who frees sinners.

—St. Alexander of Alexandria

145 O strange and inconceivable thing! We did not really die, we were not really buried, we were not really crucified and raised again. Yet our imitation is only a symbol, though our salvation is in reality. Christ was actually crucified, and actually buried, and truly rose again; and all these things have been granted to us, that we may participate in His sufferings by imitation, and might gain salvation in reality.

—St. Cyril of Jerusalem

146 O surpassing loving-kindness! Christ received the nails in His undefiled hands and feet, and He endured anguish; while to me He granted salvation, without suffering or toil, by the fellowship of His pain.

—St. Cyril of Jerusalem

147 The Cross, if you wish to define it, is the confirmation of victory, the way by which God descended to man, the trophy against material spirits, the repulsion of death, the foundation of the ascent to the true day, and the ladder for those who hurry to enjoy the light that is there.

—St. Methodius of Olympus

148 Whoever shall not confess the testimony of the Cross is the devil.

—St. Polycarp of Smyrna

149 How great a terror to the demons is this sign. See how, when adjured by Christ, they flee from the bodies which they have besieged.

—Lactantius

150 By the Sign of the Cross all magic is stopped, and all witchcraft brought to nothing.

—St. Athanasius

151 In every act we do, in every step we take, let our hand trace the Lord's Cross.

—St. Jerome

152 In all our actions, when we come in or go out, when we dress, when we wash, at our meals, before retiring to sleep, we make on our foreheads the Sign of the Cross. These practices are not committed by a formal law of Scripture, but tradition teaches them, custom confirms them, faith observes them.

—Tertullian

153 In the . . . Sign of the Cross is all virtue and power. . . . In this Sign of the Cross is salvation for all who are marked on their foreheads

—St. Cyprian of Carthage

154 By this sign the passions are truly blunted. The passion of the passions took place in the Passion, and the death of death by the death of Christ, since He was neither subdued by death, nor overcome by the pains of the Passion.

—St. Methodius of Olympus

155 He has changed sunset into sunrise, and through the Cross brought death to life. And having wrenched man from destruction, He has raised him to the skies.

—St. Clement of Alexandria

Salvation

156 Listen to the Savior: I regenerated you, unhappily born by the world to death. I set you free, I healed you, I redeemed you. I will give you life that is unending, eternal, supernatural. I will show you the face of God, the good Father.

—St. Clement of Alexandria

157 I urge you to be saved. This Christ desires.

—St. Clement of Alexandria

158 The thief was on the cross, and he was justified by a single word. And Judas, who was counted among the Apostles, lost all his labor in a single night and descended from heaven to hell. So, let no one boast of his good works, for all those who trust in themselves fall.

—Anonymous (*Sayings of the Desert Fathers*)

159 It is His will that men should praise Him with unanimity and adore Him with one consent. For this is His will in Christ, that those who are saved by Him may be many; but that you do not cause any loss or lessening to Him or to the Church, or diminish the number by one soul, destroyed by you, who might have been saved by repentance.

—Anonymous (*Teaching of the Twelve Apostles*)

160 Into the Jews' olive tree we have been grafted.

—Tertullian

161 Let the sinner rejoice, since he is invited to grace. Let the Gentiles exult, for they are called to life.

—Pope St. Leo the Great

Grace

162 When the mind is filled with divine knowledge and understanding through no agency of man or of angel, then may the mind believe that it receives the very kisses of the Word of God.

—Origen

163 There are divine gifts which God gives also to those who do not pray, such as the beginning of faith, and divine gifts which He gives only to those who pray, such as final perseverance.

—St. Augustine

164 If grace does not exist, how does He save the world? If there is no free will, how does He judge the world?

—St. Augustine

165 God is seen by those who are enabled to see Him, when they have the eyes of their soul opened. For all have eyes, but in some they are covered and do not see the light of the sun.

—St. Theophilus of Antioch

166 It was impossible for man to come to know God's ways by his own efforts. But God did not leave man to err in search of the light of wisdom, wandering through inescapable darkness with nothing to show for his labor. At last He opened his eyes, and made the investigation of the truth His own gift, so that He might show the nothingness of human wisdom, and point out to man, who was wandering in error, the way of obtaining immortality.

—Lactantius

167 Our eyes cannot frequently look upon . . . the sun. But when we look upon its splendor or its rays pouring in, perhaps, through windows or some small openings to admit the light, we can reflect how great is the supply and source of the light of the body. In the same way, the works of divine providence and the plan of this whole world are a sort of rays, as it were, of the nature of God.

—Origen

168 Many have been converted to Christianity as if against their will, some sort of spirit having suddenly transformed their minds from a hatred of the doctrine to a readiness to die in its defense.

—Origen

169 Preaching, although in itself true and most worthy of belief, is not sufficient to reach the human heart, unless a certain power be imparted to the speaker from God and a grace appear upon his words. And it is only by divine agency that this takes place in those who speak effectively.

—Origen

170 Grace cannot be unjust. Nor can justice be cruel.
—St. Augustine

171 Not all who have sight are illuminated by Christ in equal measure. Each has illumination in proportion as he has capacity to receive the power of the light. The eyes of our body do not receive the light of the sun in equal measures, but the higher the levels to which one climbs, the more lofty the viewpoint from which one watches the vista of the sunrise, and the larger is one's sense of the power of the sun's light and heat. So it is also with our spirit: the higher and the further it goes in its approach to Christ, the more nearly it exposes itself to the glory of His light, the more finely and splendidly is it illuminated by His radiance.

—Origen

172 I forget my own country, O Lord, for desire of Your grace. I forget . . . even the desire of mother and family for You, O Christ, are all things to me.

—St. Methodius of Olympus

173 To praise oneself is a hateful bragging. Yet it may not be bragging, but gratitude, to recall what is attributed not to the virtue of man, but to the blessing of God.

—St. Cyprian of Carthage

174 When God crowns our merits, he is crowning nothing other than His gifts.

—St. Augustine

The Will of God

175 Glory be to God for all things. I will never cease saying this, whatever befalls me.

—St. John Chrysostom

176 Nothing happens without God; we know this from many sources. And everyone who realizes that God is Reason, Wisdom, Perfect Goodness, and Truth — and that He could not admit of anything that is not good and not consistent with His Truth — everyone who realizes this will admit that God's dispensations have no element of chance and confusion. . . . It befits us, then to acknowledge that these things happen for the best.

—St. Gregory of Nyssa

177 A blind, meaningless event can never be the work of God; for it is the property of God, as Scripture says, to make all things in wisdom (see Ps 104:24).

—St. Gregory of Nyssa

178 You have no reason to grieve for ill success. Perhaps it has seemed good to God to make my racecourse longer, so that my crown may be brighter.

—St. John Chrysostom

179 I do not despair of happier times, considering that at the helm of the universe is He who overcomes the storm not by human skill, but by His *fiat*.

—St. John Chrysostom

180 Your will should be corrected to become identified with God's will. You must not bend God's will to suit yours.

—St. Augustine

181 To serve God is nothing other than maintaining and preserving justice by good works.

—Lactantius

182 What then, is more precious than to be in the hand of God? For God is Life and Light, and those who are in God's hand are in life and light.

—St. John of Damascus

Divine Mercy

183 Even if we have thousands of acts of great virtue to our credit, our confidence in being heard must be based on God's mercy and His love for men. Even if we stand at the very summit of virtue, it is by mercy that we shall be saved.

—St. John Chrysostom

184 It is impossible that He Who holds perfect excellence should not also possess perfect patience.

—Lactantius

185 The Christian life is the true Jacob's ladder on which the angels ascend and descend. Meanwhile, the Lord stands above, holding out His hand to those who slip, sustaining by His vision the weary steps of those who ascend.

—St. Jerome

186 Most gently, the finger of Your justice, in love and compassion, touches the wounds of him who is to be healed.

—St. Ephrem of Syria

187 Those who know that His voice is gentle and pleasing are those who have welcomed the grace of the Gospel.

—St. Gregory of Nyssa

188 Why rely on yourself and fall? Cast yourself upon His arm. Be not afraid. He will not let you slip. Cast yourself in confidence. He will receive you and heal you.

—St. Augustine

Baptism

189 In the bath of saving water, the fire of hell is extinguished.

—St. Cyprian of Carthage

190 Being baptized, we are illuminated. Illuminated, we become sons. Made sons, we are made perfect. Made perfect, we are made immortal.

—St. Clement of Alexandria

191 We little fish, like our Fish, Jesus Christ, are born in water, and it is only by living in water that we are safe.

—Tertullian

192 The flesh is washed so that the soul may be cleansed.

—Tertullian

193 The Church has received from the Apostles the custom of administering baptism even to infants. For those who have been entrusted with the secrets of the divine mysteries knew very well that all are tainted with the stain of original sin, which must be washed off by water and the Spirit.

—Origen

194 By having the water thrice poured on us and ascending again up from the water, we enact that saving burial and resurrection which took place on the third day. We do so with this thought in our mind, that as we have power over the water, both to be in it and arise out of it, so He, too, who has the universe at His sovereign disposal, immersed Himself in death, as we in the water, to return to His own blessedness.

—St. Gregory of Nyssa

195 I was dead, but because in baptism I died together with Christ, I received the light of life from Christ. And he who dies in Christ, being warmed by Christ, receives the breath of life and resurrection.

—St. Ambrose of Milan

196 You died and were born at the same time. The saving water became for you both a tomb and a mother.

—St. Cyril of Jerusalem

197 The baptismal pool of the Trinity is a workshop for the salvation of all those who believe. It frees from the serpent sting all those who are washed therein, and, remaining a virgin, becomes the mother of all through the Holy Spirit.

—Didymus the Blind

198 For when we are immersed in the baptismal pool, we are by the goodness of God the Father and through the grace of His Holy Spirit stripped of our sins. We are regenerated and sealed by His own kingly power as we lay aside the old man.

—Didymus the Blind

199 When we come up out of the pool, we put on Christ our Savior, as an incorruptible garment, worthy of the same honor as the Holy Spirit who regenerated us and marked us with His seal.

—Didymus the Blind

200 Those who suffered martyrdom before baptism, having been washed in their own blood, were vivified by the Holy Spirit of God.

—Didymus the Blind

201 Thus, renovated in baptism, we enjoy the familiarity of God, in so far as the powers of our nature permit.

—Didymus the Blind

202 Do not think of the font as filled with ordinary water, but think rather of the spiritual grace that is given with the water.

—St. Cyril of Jerusalem

203 We call something perfect when it lacks nothing. And what is yet wanting to him who knows God?

—St. Clement of Alexandria

204 The new man, born again and restored to God by grace, says "Father!" because he has now begun to be a son.

—St. Cyprian of Carthage

205 Already you stand on the frontier of mystery!

—St. Cyril of Jerusalem

Eucharist

206 The flesh feeds on the Body and Blood of Christ, that the soul may grow fat on God.

—Tertullian

207 Christ, indeed, gave even His flesh, by which those who believe are nourished, like little children.

—Hippolytus of Rome

208 What seems bread is not bread, though bread by taste; but the Body of Christ. What seems wine is not wine, though the taste will have it so; but the Blood of Christ.

—St. Cyril of Jerusalem

209 The Lord Jesus Himself proclaims: "This is My Body" (Mt 26:26). Before the blessing of the heavenly words, another nature is spoken of; after the consecration, the Body is signified. He Himself speaks of His Blood. Before the consecration, it has another name; after, it is called Blood. And you say: "Amen," that is, "It is true." Let the heart within confess what the mouth utters; let the soul feel what the voice speaks.

—St. Ambrose of Milan

210 The food that has been made the Eucharist by the prayer of His Word, and which nourishes our flesh and blood by assimilation, is both the Flesh and Blood of that Jesus Who was made flesh.

—St. Justin Martyr

211 As long as the invocation and prayers have not begun, there is only bread and wine. But after the great and wonderful prayers have been pronounced, then the bread becomes the Body of Our Lord Jesus Christ, and the wine becomes His Blood. Let us come to the celebration of the mysteries!

—St. Athanasius

212 The sacrament you receive is made what it is by the Word of Christ. If the word of Elijah had such power as to bring down fire from heaven, shall not the Word of Christ have power to change the nature of the elements?

—St. Ambrose of Milan

213 If I am asked how bread is changed into the Body of Christ, I answer: "The Holy Ghost overshadows the priest and operates in the same manner in the elements which He effected in the womb of the Virgin Mary."

—St. John of Damascus

214 Once, in Cana of Galilee, He turned water into wine, akin to blood. Is it incredible that He should have turned wine into blood? When called to a bodily marriage, He miraculously wrought that wonderful work; yet, on the children of the bride-chamber, shall He not much rather be acknowledged to have bestowed the fruition of His Body and Blood?

—St. Cyril of Jerusalem

215 Consider, then, the bread and wine not as bare elements. They are, according to the Lord's declaration, the Body and Blood of Christ. For even though sense suggests this to you, let faith assure you. Judge not the matter from the taste, but be fully assured by faith, without misgiving.

—St. Cyril of Jerusalem

216 Given to you in the figure of bread is His Body, and in the figure of wine His Blood; that you, by partaking of the Body and Blood of Christ, may be made of the same body and the same blood with Him. For thus we come to bear Christ in us, because His Body and Blood are distributed through our members; thus it is that, according to St. Peter, we became partakers of the divine nature (see 2 Peter 1:4).

—St. Cyril of Jerusalem

217 Not only ought we to see the Lord, but we ought to take Him in our hands, eat Him, set our teeth upon His Flesh, and most intimately unite ourselves with Him.

—St. John Chrysostom

218 Reflect, O man, what sacrificial flesh you take in your hand — and to what table you will approach. Remember that you, though dust and ashes, do receive the Blood and the Body of Christ.

—St. John Chrysostom

219 What the Lord did not tolerate on the Cross, He tolerates now in the sacrifice through the love of you. He permits Himself to be broken in pieces that all may be filled to satiety.

—St. John Chrysostom

220 If anyone gave you grains of gold, would not you hold them with all care, on your guard against losing any?

Will you not keep watch more carefully, then, that not a crumb fall from you of what is more precious than gold and precious stones?

—St. Cyril of Jerusalem

221 There is one Christ everywhere, complete both in this world and in the other; one body. Though offered in many places, He is but one body so there is but one sacrifice. . . . We offer now what was offered then.

—St. John Chrysostom

222 The Lord's passion is the sacrifice we offer.

—St. Cyprian of Carthage

223 Believe that now the same banquet takes place as when Christ sat at table, and that this banquet is in no way different.

—St. John Chrysostom

224 In this very sacrament, our people are shown to be made one. Just as many grains, collected and ground and mixed together, make one bread, so in Christ, who is heavenly bread, we may know that there is one body, with which our number is joined and united.

—St. Cyprian of Carthage

225 Take care, then, to have but one Eucharist. For there is one Flesh of our Lord Jesus Christ, and one cup to show forth the unity of His Blood; one altar, as there is one bishop, along with the priests and deacons, my fellow-servants.

—St. Ignatius of Antioch

226 The Eucharist is a safeguard to those who receive. We need it in order to arm, with the protection of the Lord's abundance, those whom we wish to keep safe against the adversary.

—St. Cyprian of Carthage

227 How can they say that the flesh, which is nourished with the Body of the Lord and with His Blood, goes to corruption and does not partake of life? . . . The bread, which is produced from the earth, receives the invocation of God, and is no longer common bread but the Eucharist, consisting of two realities, earthly and heavenly. So also our bodies, when they receive the Eucharist, are no longer corruptible, having the hope of the resurrection to eternity.

—St. Irenaeus of Lyons

228 Truly, in that most awesome hour [of the liturgy], we should have our hearts on high with God, and not below, thinking of earth and earthly things. The Priest bids all in that hour to dismiss all cares of this life, or household worries, and to have their hearts in heaven with the merciful God.

—St. Cyril of Jerusalem

229 Do not separate yourselves from Communion; do not deprive yourselves, by the pollution of sins, of these holy and spiritual mysteries.

—St. Cyril of Jerusalem

230 We ask that this bread should be given to us daily, that we who are in Christ and daily receive the Eucharist as food of salvation, may not by heinous sin . . . be prevented from partaking of the heavenly bread, may not be separated from Christ's Body.

—St. Cyprian of Carthage

231 It is good and beneficial to take Communion every day, and to partake of the Holy Body and Blood of Christ. For He distinctly says, "He who eats My Flesh and drinks My Blood has eternal life" (Jn 6:54). And who doubts that to share frequently in life is the same thing as to have abundant life?

—St. Basil the Great

232 Every soul that receives the bread come down from heaven is a "house of bread" [in Hebrew, *Bethlehem*], the bread of Christ, being nourished and having its heart strengthened by the support of that heavenly bread that dwells within it.

—St. Ambrose of Milan

233 The Body of Christ in the Eucharist demands pure souls, not costly garments.

—St. John Chrysostom

234 The angel could not touch the fire's coal with his fingers, but just brought it close to Isaiah's mouth. The angel did not hold it, and Isaiah did not consume it, but Our Lord has allowed us to do both.

—St. Ephrem of Syria

Confession

235 The confession of evil works is the first beginning of good works.

—St. Augustine

236 He who confesses his sins freely receives pardon from the priest by virtue of the grace of Christ.

—St. Athanasius

237 Each one should confess his own sin, while he who has sinned is still in this world, while his confession may be received, while the satisfaction and the remission made by the priests are pleasing to the Lord.

—St. Cyprian of Carthage

238 Confession heals, confession justifies, confession grants pardon of sin. All hope consists in confession. In confession there is a chance for mercy. Believe it firmly, do not doubt, do not hesitate, never despair of the mercy of God.

—St. Isidore of Seville

239 On the Lord's Day, gather together to break bread and offer thanks. But confess your sins first, so that your sacrifice may be pure.

—Anonymous (*Teaching of the Twelve Apostles*)

240 Those who become filthy after the grace of baptism may once more be cleansed.

—St. Cyprian of Carthage

241 Confess what you have done in word or deed, by night or day. Confess in an acceptable time, and in the day of salvation receive the heavenly treasure.

—St. Cyril of Jerusalem

242 It is not enough to remove the arrow from the body; we also have to heal the wound caused by the arrow. It is the same with the soul. After we have received forgiveness for our sins, we have to heal the wound that remains through penance.

—St. John Chrysostom

Priests of God

243 The Church is composed of the bishop, the clergy, and all who are steadfast.

—St. Cyprian of Carthage

244 The Church, which is catholic and one, is not split asunder nor divided, but is truly bound and joined together by the cement of its priests, who hold fast to one another.

—St. Cyprian of Carthage

245 The dominion of the priest lies in his helplessness, as it is said: "When I am weak, then I am strong."

—St. Ambrose of Milan

246 Avoid, like the plague, a clergyman who is also a businessman.

—St. Jerome

247 Christ was sent forth by God, and the Apostles by Christ. Both these appointments were made in an orderly way, according to the will of God. Thus, they went forth proclaiming that the kingdom of God was at hand. . . . And thus preaching through countries and cities, they appointed the first fruits of their labors (having first proved them by the Spirit) to be bishops and deacons of those who should afterwards believe.

—Pope St. Clement I of Rome

248 As the Lord was united to the Father and did nothing without Him . . . so neither should you do anything without the bishop and priests. . . . Let there be one prayer, one supplication, one mind, one hope, in love and in joy undefiled. There is one Jesus Christ, and nothing is more excellent than He. Come together, then, as into one temple of God, to one altar, to one Jesus Christ, who came forth from one Father, and is with one, and has gone to one.

—St. Ignatius of Antioch

249 Wherever the bishop shall appear, there let the multitude also be; even as wherever Jesus Christ is, there is the Catholic Church.

—St. Ignatius of Antioch

250 You should understand that the bishop is in the Church and the Church is in the bishop and that whoever is not with the bishop is not in the Church.

—St. Cyprian of Carthage

251 The bishop is the minister of the Word, the keeper of knowledge, the mediator between God and you in the various parts of your divine worship. He is the teacher of piety; and, next after God, he is your father, who has begotten you again to the adoption of sons by water and the Spirit.

—Anonymous (*Teaching of the Twelve Apostles*)

252 Let a man respect his bishop. For whoever is sent by the Master to run His house, we ought to receive him as we would receive the Master Himself.

—St. Ignatius of Antioch

253 Persist in the true faith and make your life firm on the rock of the Church — that is, on the confession of the blessed Peter, Prince of the Apostles.

—Pope St. Gregory the Great

254 The primacy is given to Peter that it may be shown that the Church is one and the See of Christ is one.

—St. Cyprian of Carthage

255 Rome has spoken; the matter is settled.

—St. Augustine

256 Peter has spoken through Leo. . . . Anathema to him who teaches otherwise.

—Pope St. Leo the Great

Prayer

257 Ask constantly, not by composing endless prayers, but rather telling Him of our needs with simplicity.

—St. John Chrysostom

258 Prayer is conversation with God.

—St. Clement of Alexandria

259 [Christians] walk on earth, but their conversation is in heaven.

—Anonymous (*Letter to Diognetus*)

260 Prayer is the raising of the mind to God and the asking of good things.

—St. John of Damascus

261 To pray much is to knock for Him to Whom we pray, with prolonged and pious exercise of the heart. This is often done more by groans than speeches, by weeping than by addresses.

—St. Augustine

262 When we leave the roof that shelters us, prayer should be our armor; and when we return from the street we should pray before we sit down, and not give the frail body rest until the soul is fed.

—St. Jerome

263 The star of morn to night succeeds;
We therefore meekly pray,
May God in all our words and deeds,

Keep us from harm this day;
May He in love restrain us still
From tones of strife and words of ill,
And wrap around and close our eyes
To earth's absorbing vanities.

—St. Ambrose of Milan

264 It is good, before we take food, to bless the Maker of all things, and to sing when we drink.

—St. Clement of Alexandria

265 No meal should be begun without prayer, and before leaving table thanks should be returned to the Creator.

—St. Jerome

266 Before every endeavor, but especially if the subject is divinity, we must begin with prayer.

—Pseudo-Dionysius the Areopagite

267 Pious exercises nourish the soul with divine thoughts.

—St. Basil the Great

268 If a man wants God to hear his prayer quickly, then before he prays for anything else, even his own soul, when he stands and stretches out his hands towards God, he must pray with all his heart for his enemies. Through this action God will hear everything that he asks.

—Anonymous (*Sayings of the Desert Fathers*)

269 I guard you from those beasts in the shape of men, whom you must not receive, and, if possible, not even meet with. Still, you must pray to God for them, that they may be brought to repentance. That will be difficult, but

Jesus Christ, who is our true life, has the power to accomplish it.

—St. Ignatius of Antioch

270 Even if God does not immediately give us what we ask, even if many people try to put us off our prayers, let us still go on praying.

—St. John Chrysostom

271 May God hear you. He is able to do more than we ask or understand.

—St. Augustine

272 How many . . . are at this hour communing with God, and embracing Him, and detaining Him, while you are deprived of so great light, enfeebled as you are with lazy sleep!

—St. John Cassian

273 At the moment of prayer, chase from your spirit even the simple representations of human realities and the images of all creatures. Or the imagination, being occupied with objects of less importance, will lose Him Who is incomparably superior to them all.

—St. Maximus the Confessor

274 Usually our intellect endures prayer impatiently, because of its narrow and constricted capacity for prayer, but gladly gives itself up to theology because of the freedom and the expanse of its speculation about God. Therefore, in order not to give free rein to its longing — and even to prevent it, in its enthusiasm, from overreaching itself unreasonably — let us give as much time as possible to prayer, to the recitation of psalms, to reading the

Scriptures, without, however, neglecting the speculations of scientific men whose faith is demonstrated by their word.

—Diodicus

275 There is no need at all to make long discourses; it is enough to stretch out one's hands and say, "Lord, as You will, and as You know, have mercy." And if the conflict grows fiercer say, "Lord, help!" He knows very well what we need and He shows us His mercy.

—Anonymous (*Sayings of the Desert Fathers*)

276 To sing is to pray twice.

—St. Augustine

277 O, the beauty of those who sing of the mysteries of God! May I, too, join in these songs in my prayer. . . . Do not shun a spiritual hymn, nor be ill-disposed to listen to it.

—St. Methodius of Olympus

278 Soothing hymns compose the mind to a cheerful and calm state.

—St. Basil the Great

279 Be like the grasshopper and make night musical. . . . Sing with the spirit, but sing with the understanding, too. And let your song be that of the psalmist.

—St. Jerome

280 We meet together as an assembly and congregation, that, offering up a united prayer, we may wrestle with Him in our supplications. This violence God delights in.

—Tertullian

281 It is neither wrong nor unprofitable to spend much time in praying, if there is leisure for this without hindering other good and necessary works to which duty calls us.

—St. Augustine

282   Now that the daylight dies away,
By all Thy grace and love,
Thee, Maker of the world, we pray
To watch our bed above.
Let dreams depart and phantoms fly,
The offspring of the night,
Keep us, like shrines, beneath Thine eye,
Pure in our foe's despite.

—St. Ambrose of Milan

Presence of God

283 Wherever you may be, God will come to you, if the chambers of your soul be found of such a sort that He can dwell in you.

—St. Gregory of Nyssa

284 Let us reflect how near He is, and that none of the thoughts or reasonings in which we engage are hid from Him.

—Pope St. Clement I of Rome

285 The Trinity is near to all things, and yet not all things are near to It.

—Pseudo-Dionysius the Areopagite

286 Let us consider how we ought to conduct ourselves in the sight of the Godhead and of His angels, and let us sing the psalms in such a way that our mind may be in harmony with our voice.

—St. Benedict of Nursia

287 Let Him, the ever-living God, be constantly present to your mind. For your mind itself is His likeness: it, too, is invisible and impalpable, and not to be represented by any form, yet by its will does the whole body move.

—St. Melito of Sardis

288 We shall be His temples, and He will be our God within us.

—St. Ignatius of Antioch

289 You are all fellow travelers, God-bearers and temple-bearers, Christ-bearers.

—St. Ignatius of Antioch

290 Let us do all things in the conviction that He dwells in us.

—St. Ignatius of Antioch

291 If the mere presence of an important person who is worthy of respect is enough to improve the behavior of the people before him, how is it that the continual presence of God . . . does not increasingly better us in our speech, actions, and feelings?

—St. Clement of Alexandria

292 Be of good cheer, only work, only strive cheerfully; for nothing is lost. Every prayer of yours, every psalm you sing is recorded. Every alms, every fast is recorded. Every marriage duly observed is recorded.

—St. Cyril of Jerusalem

293 But as you have gladly listened to the good things, listen without shrinking to the contrary. Every covetous deed of yours is recorded. Every fleshly deed, every perjury, every blasphemy, every sorcery, every theft, every murder. All these are recorded.

—St. Cyril of Jerusalem

294 If you keep your inner man full of wicked thoughts, even if you were on Golgotha, even if you were on the Mount of Olives, even if you stood on the memorial rock of the Resurrection, you will be as far away from receiving Christ into yourself as one who has not even begun to confess Him.

—St. Gregory of Nyssa

295 The all-seeing God knows how many stones have been flung at me.

—Theodoret of Cyrrhus

296 We believe that the divine presence is everywhere and that "the eyes of the Lord are looking on the good and the evil in every place." But we should believe this especially without any doubt when we are assisting at the work of God.

—St. Benedict of Nursia

297 We must be eager to be near the good God, to be always with the Lord. We must never deserve to be ranked among the wicked.

—Pseudo-Dionysius the Areopagite

298 Keep close to Jesus.

—Anonymous (*Sayings of the Desert Fathers*)

Worship

299 If anyone should ask a truly wise man why he was born, he will answer without fear or hesitation, that he was born for the purpose of worshiping God.

—Lactantius

300 Piety is nothing other than the recognition of God as Father.

—Lactantius

301 Not that He needs our supplications or loves to see the homage of so many thousands laid at His feet. This is for our benefit, and works to our advantage.

—Arnobius

302 We the faithful do not worship images as gods, as did the heathen Greeks — God forbid! — but our only purpose and desire is to see in the image a reflection of the facial form of the Beloved.

—St. Athanasius

303 If the honor paid to Him is shared by idols, He altogether ceases to be worshiped, since His religion requires us to believe that He is the one and only God.

—Lactantius

304 Worship a living being, that you may live; for he must necessarily die who has subjected himself and his soul to the dead.

—Lactantius

305 In former times, God being without form or body, could in no way be represented. But today, since God has appeared in the flesh and lived among men, I can represent what is visible in God. I do not worship matter, but I worship the Creator of matter Who became matter for my sake . . . and Who, through matter accomplished my salvation.

—St. John of Damascus

306 Discern between the different kinds of worship. Abraham bowed down to the sons of Hamor, men who had neither faith nor knowledge of God . . . Jacob bowed to the ground before Esau, his brother, and also before the tip of his son Joseph's staff. He bowed down, but he did not adore. Joshua . . . and Daniel bowed in veneration before an angel of God, but they did not adore him. For adoration is one thing, and that which is offered in order to honor something of great excellence is another.

—St. John of Damascus

307 No one may whisper, nor slumber, nor laugh, nor nod; for, in church, all ought to stand wisely, soberly, and attentively, having their attention fixed upon the Word of the Lord.

—Anonymous (*Teaching of the Twelve Apostles*)

308 O King Supreme . . . forgive those who fly from the worship of Your name and the observance of Your religion. It is no wonder that You are unknown. It is a cause of greater astonishment if You are clearly comprehended.

—Arnobius

Contemplation

309 Do not go outside, but return into yourself, for the truth dwells in the interior man.

—St. Augustine

310 The love of the truth seeks out the quiet of contemplation.

—St. Augustine

311 No one should be so active as not to seek the contemplation of God.

—St. Augustine

312 In order to deliver the spirit so perfectly from the passions that it can pray without distractions, the active way is not enough, unless it is followed by various spiritual contemplations.

—St. Maximus the Confessor

313 The contemplation of God is the reverence and worship of the common Father of mankind.

—Lactantius

314 The birds and almost all of dumb creation see the heavens, but it is given to us uniquely to behold the heaven as we stand erect, that we may seek religion there; that, since we cannot see God with our eyes, we may contemplate Him with our mind in the place where He keeps His throne.

—Lactantius

315 We cannot possibly scorn the gratification of food given to us, unless the mind is fixed on the contemplation of divine things, and is entranced instead with the love of virtue and the delight of things celestial.

—St. John Cassian

316 A man will despise all things present as transitory when he has securely fixed his mental gaze on those things that are immovable and eternal, and already contemplates in heart — though still in the flesh — the blessedness of his future life.

—St. John Cassian

317 If you discover that your nature is changeable, transcend yourself.

—St. Augustine

318 No one should be so contemplative as to forget in the course of his contemplation that he must be of service to his neighbor.

—St. Augustine

319 How wondrous that the mind should gather all its forces to break through and gaze upon Your Light.

—St. Ephrem of Syria

Intercession

320 Urge those who have familiar speech with God to use much prayer, with much perseverance, for the stilling of the tempest that is now wrecking the whole world.

—St. John Chrysostom

321 We pray, too, for the emperors, for their ministers and for all in authority, for the welfare of the world, for the prevalence of peace, for the delay of the final consummation.

—Tertullian

322 It is through the monks that the world is kept in being and that through them also human life is preserved and honored by God. . . . There is no town or village in Egypt that is not surrounded by hermitages as if by walls, and all the people depend on the prayers of the monks as if on God Himself.

—Anonymous (*Sayings of the Desert Fathers*)

323 Let us pray for those who have fallen into any sin, that meekness and humility may be given to them, so that they may submit, not to us, but to the will of God.

—Pope St. Clement I of Rome

324 The poor are my defenders, but it is by their prayers. Blind though they be, lame, feeble, and aged, yet they have a strength greater than that of the stoutest warriors.

—St. Ambrose of Milan

325 We must always be assisted in obtaining God's mercy by the prayers of special intercessors, that we may be raised by the Apostles' merits in proportion as we are weighed down by our own sins.

—Pope St. Leo the Great

326 Pray also for kings and powers and rulers, and for those who persecute and hate you, and for the enemies of the Cross, that your fruit may be manifest unto all, that you may be perfect in Him.

—St. Polycarp of Smyrna

327 The world continues to exist only because of the prayers of supplication of the Christians.

—Aristides of Athens

328 Our prayer is public and common. When we pray, we pray not for one, but for the whole people, because we the whole people are one.

—St. Cyprian of Carthage

329 Let us be mutually mindful of one another, of one heart and one mind. Let us ever pray for one another, and by mutual love lighten our burdens and difficulties. And if one of us should, by the swiftness of divine action, depart from here first, let our love continue in the presence of the Lord. Let not prayer for our brothers and sisters cease in the presence of the mercy of the Father.

—St. Cyprian of Carthage

Fasting

330 A clear rule for self-control handed down by the Fathers is this: stop eating while still hungry.

—St. John Cassian

331 The duty of fasting is rendered acceptable to God when it is made perfect by the fruits of charity.

—St. John Cassian

332 Fasting is better than prayer, but almsgiving is better than both.

—Pseudo-Clement

333 Feed prayer on fastings.

—Tertullian

334 We do not urge you to immoderate fasting, or an extravagant abstinence from food. This breaks delicate frames and makes them sickly, before the foundation of holy conversation is yet laid.

—St. Jerome

335 You should fast short of panting and failing in breath, and of being carried off or led by your companions — enough to subdue your appetite, while you are still able to attend to sacred reading, psalms, and the usual vigils.

—St. Jerome

336 Fasting is not an absolute virtue, but the foundation of other virtues.

—St. Jerome

337 The canonical observance of fasts is valuable and by all means to be kept. But unless this is followed by a temperate partaking of food, one will not be able to arrive at the goal of perfection.

—St. John Cassian

338 Perfection of mind depends upon the abstinence of the belly.

—St. John Cassian

339 Severe fasting is rendered useless if followed by unnecessary relaxation, and leads to the vice of gluttony.

—St. John Cassian

340 A reasonable supply of food, taken daily in moderation, is better than a severe and long fast at intervals.

—St. John Cassian

341 Excessive fasting has been known not only to undermine the constancy of the mind, but also to weaken the power of prayers through sheer weariness of body.

—St. John Cassian

342 When any of the brethren arrive, we ought to show the virtues of kindness and charity instead of observing a severe abstinence and our strict daily rule. Nor should we consider our own wishes, profit, or the ardor of our desires. Instead, we should set before us and gladly fulfill whatever refreshment the guest may demand from us.

—St. John Cassian

343 Receiving Christ in you, I ought to refresh Him. But when I have sent you on your way, I shall be able to balance the hospitality offered for His sake by a stricter fast on my own account.

—St. John Cassian

344 A monk ought to bestow attention on his fasts, just as if he were going to remain in the flesh for a hundred years; and to curb the motions of the soul, and to forget injuries, and to loathe sadness, and despise sorrows and losses, as if he were daily at the point of death.

—St. John Cassian

The Heart

345 If you have a heart, you can be saved.

—Anonymous (*Sayings of the Desert Fathers*)

346 Man's heart is no small thing, for it can embrace so much.

—Origen

347 No one understands in heart . . . unless he be open-minded and completely attentive.

—Origen

348 Preparing the heart is the unlearning of the prejudices of evil converse. It is like smoothing the waxen tablet before attempting to write on it.

—St. Basil the Great

349 Christ makes the bitterness of the human heart sweet by the sweetness of His Word.

—Hippolytus of Rome

350 Just as a lamp lights up a dark room, so the fear of God when it penetrates the heart of a man illuminates him, teaching him all the virtues and commandments of God.

—Anonymous (*Sayings of the Desert Fathers*)

351 If a man's heart has been purified . . . he will see the image of the divine nature in his own beauty.

—St. Gregory of Nyssa

352 Where should my heart flee from my heart? Where should I flee from myself?

—St. Augustine

353 It is not so much the corruptible flesh as the clean heart, which is made a shrine for God, and a temple of the Holy Ghost.

—St. John Cassian

354 Because you are cleansed, you are able to perceive what is invisible to those who are not purified. The darkness caused by material entanglements has been removed from the eyes of your soul, and so you see the blessed vision radiant in the pure heaven of your heart..

—St. Gregory of Nyssa

355 Abba Lot went to see Abba Joseph and said to him, "Abba, as far as I can, I say my little office, I fast a little, I pray and meditate, I live in peace and as far as I can, I purify my thoughts. What else can I do?" Then the old man stood up and stretched his hands towards heaven. His fingers became like ten lamps of fire and he said to him, "If you will, you can become all flame."

—Anonymous (*Sayings of the Desert Fathers*)

The Body

356 The human body is a revelation of the goodness of God and the providence of the body's Creator.

—St. Augustine

357 The body is a hidden temple, and the heart a hidden altar.

—Anonymous (*Liber Graduum*)

358 We profess that the whole nature of the body comes from God, its almighty creator.

—St. Augustine

359 Let that handiwork be forever glorified that became the cloak of its own creator.

—St. John Chrysostom

360 Flesh did not diminish the glory of the Word; far be the thought. On the contrary, it was glorified by Him.

—St. Athanasius

361 The chief good of the body is not bodily pleasure, not absence of pain, not strength, not beauty, not swiftness, or whatever else is usually reckoned among the goods of the body, but simply the soul.

—St. Augustine

362 If the body should overpower the soul and subject it to its dominion, it is in everlasting darkness and death.

—Lactantius

363 It is an impossibility that the fiery motions of the body can be extinguished before the incentives of the other chief vices are utterly rooted out.

—St. John Cassian

364 Of what use to your salvation is all the anxious care you spend in arranging your hair?

—Tertullian

365 Your only pleasures are the most sensual pleasures of the body. Your life is the life of a sea anemone.

—Synesius of Cyrene

The Tongue

366 Restrain your tongue from cursing, because with it you adore the Lord.

—Commodianus

367 Slander is worse than cannibalism.

—St. John Chrysostom

368 Beware also of a babbling tongue and of itching ears. Neither detract from others nor listen to detractors.

—St. Jerome

369 The chatty old woman, the doting old man, and the wordy sophist — all take up the Scriptures, tear them in pieces, and teach them before they have learned them.

—St. Jerome

370 Men who charm the popular ear by the polish of their style suppose every word they say to be a law of God.

—St. Jerome

371 Do not be hasty with your tongue, for the mouth is a snare of death.

—Pseudo-Barnabas

372 Whenever we cover our brother's sin, God will cover ours; whenever we tell people about our brother's guilt, God will do the same about ours.

—Anonymous (*Sayings of the Desert Fathers*)

373 We knew an old man, Machetes by name, who lived at a distance from the crowds of the brethren, and obtained by his daily prayers this grace from the Lord, that as often as a spiritual conference was held, whether by day or by night, he was never overcome by sleep. But if any one tried to introduce a word of detraction, or idle talk, he dropped off to sleep at once — as if the poison of slander could not possibly penetrate to pollute his ears.

—St. John Cassian

374 "Be still, and know that I am God," says the Scripture (Ps 46:10). Excuse yourself from speaking many idle words. Neither backbite, nor lend a willing ear to backbiters; but rather be prompt to prayer.

—St. Cyril of Jerusalem

375 If you speak evil in truth, that is also a crime.

—St. John Chrysostom

376 Rumor — even when it brings some truth with it — is never free from the flaw of falsehood, for it ever takes away from, adds to, and alters the truth.

—Tertullian

377 Why do we complain about God, Who has more reason to complain about all of us?

—Salvian

378 Let none lay the hand of detraction or vituperation or indiscretion or dishonor on the Lord's anointed, or on the preachers of holy Church, since vexation or detraction of them touches Christ, in whose stead they fill the office of legates in the Church.

—Pope St. Gregory the Great

Freedom

379 See how the Father attracts. He delights in teaching, and not in imposing necessity on men.

—St. Augustine

380 He who is good is free, even if he is a slave. He who is evil is a slave, even if he is a king.

—St. Augustine

381 If we are brought to Christ by force, we believe without wanting to. This is violence, not freedom.

—St. Augustine

382 He who created you without your cooperation does not justify you without your cooperation. He created you without your knowing it; He does not justify you without your wanting it.

—St. Augustine

383 Christians are forbidden to correct the stumblings of sinners by force. . . . It is necessary to make a man better not by force but by persuasion. We neither have authority granted us by law to restrain sinners, nor, if it were, should we know how to use it, since God gives the crown to those who are kept from evil not by force, but by choice.

—St. John Chrysostom

384 It depends on us whether we wish to be saved.

—Anonymous (*Sayings of the Desert Fathers*)

385 In all our actions, God considers the intention: whether we act for Him or for some other motive.

—St. Maximus the Confessor

386 There is nothing to keep you from changing your evil way of life. You are a free man.

—St. Melito of Sardis

387 Not only in faith, but also in works, God has given man freedom of the will.

—St. Irenaeus

388 The power of choosing good and evil is within the reach of all.

—Origen

389 If we are mere instruments of heavenly cycles, then we do not have free will. And if man loses freedom, he loses everything.

—St. Gregory of Nyssa

390 There is only one good that will be free and secure from restraint or capture: a mind raised up to Christ.

—St. Gregory Nazianzen

391 Free will is not taken away because it is assisted, but is assisted in order that it not be taken away.

—St. Augustine

Sin

392 Upon every soul, sin sets its mark, and all alike it devoted to death.

—St. Melito of Sardis

393 God has created me with free will. If I have sinned, I have sinned. . . . I, not fate, not chance, not the devil.

—St. Augustine

394 We sin from two causes: either from not seeing what we ought to do, or from not doing what we see ought to be done.

—St. Augustine

395 Sin: a thought, a form, a fascination, a fall.

—St. Augustine

396 All sin is a kind of lying.

—St. Augustine

397 He who sets himself to do evil, and yet wishes others to be silent, is a witness against himself, for he wishes himself to be loved more than the truth.

—Pope St. Gregory the Great

398 Every sin is injury more to him who does it than to him who suffers it.

—St. Augustine

399 It is no fault of Christianity if a hypocrite falls into sin.

—St. Jerome

400 Sins that are easiest to amend bring the greatest punishment.

—St. John Chrysostom

401 If you cannot clear yourself of guilt, do not add to your sins.

—St. Melito of Sardis

402 We may not sin to prevent another's sinning.

—St. Augustine

403 No one sins by an act he cannot avoid.

—St. Augustine

404 The law detects sin; only grace conquers it.

—St. Augustine

405 The prime cause of certitude is sin.

—St. Augustine

406 Prosperous sinners fare worst of all in the end.

—St. John Chrysostom

407 O ungrateful and impious age, prepared for its own destruction by its extraordinary stubbornness! If a physician had come to you from strange and distant lands, offering some medicine to keep you free from every kind of disease and sickness, wouldn't you eagerly hasten to him?

—Arnobius

408 It is our sins that make the barbarians strong, our vices that vanquish Rome's soldiers: and, as if there were too little material here for carnage, civil wars have made almost greater havoc among us than the swords of foreign foes.

—St. Jerome

409 If you hear an evil report from truthful men who do not deceive, pour out your tears that you may quench the fire that burns in others. . . . Let your dwelling be in mourning, for him who is lost in sin, that he may turn back in repentance.

—St. Ephrem of Syria

410 Let us also pray for those who have fallen into any sin, that meekness and humility may be given to them, so that they may submit, not to us, but to the will of God.

—Pope St. Clement I of Rome

411 If you have accused me rightly, pray for my escape from the sin that you discern in my conduct.

—St. Basil the Great

412 Wretch that I am! I have not remembered how God observes the mind and hears the voice of the soul. I turned consciously to sin, saying to myself that God is merciful and will bear with me. And when I was not instantly struck down, I did not stop, but rather despised His forbearance and exhausted the patience of God.

—Peter of Alexandria

413 Let every man daily take an accounting with himself of the day's and the night's doings, and if he has sinned, let him stop sinning, and if he has not, let him not boast of it. . . . Let this observation be a safeguard against sinning: let us note and write down our actions and impulses of the soul as though we were to report them to each other.

—St. Anthony of Egypt

414 Ask yourselves now, I beg you, if you have come to the feast wearing your wedding garment.

—Pope St. Gregory the Great

415 Let us ask pardon for our waywardness and for what we have done yielding to any wiles of the adversary.

—Pope St. Clement of Rome

416 It is better for a man to make a clean breast of his failings than to harden his heart in imitation of those who hardened their hearts and rebelled against God's servant, Moses.

—Pope St. Clement of Rome

Repentance

417 You who are a sinner like myself, hurry to embrace repentance, as a shipwrecked man the protection of some plank.

—Tertullian

418 The heavens and angels who are there, are glad at a man's repentance.

—Tertullian

419 Repentance is the renewal of baptism. Repentance is a contract with God for a second life.

—St. John of the Ladder

420 A penitent is a buyer of humility.

—St. John of the Ladder

421 Repentance is . . . carefree self-care.

—St. John of the Ladder

422 Repentance is the daughter of hope and the renunciation of despair.

—St. John of the Ladder

423 A penitent is an undisgraced convict.

—St. John of the Ladder

424 Repentance is reconciliation with the Lord by the practice of good deeds contrary to the sins.

—St. John of the Ladder

425 If anyone is holy, let him advance. If anyone is not, let him be converted.

—Anonymous (*Teaching of the Twelve Apostles*)

426 When day begins to dawn, all together, as with one mouth and one heart, lift up to the Lord the psalm of confession, each making the words of repentance his own.

—St. Basil the Great

427 I consider those fallen mourners more blessed than those who have not fallen and are not mourning over themselves; because as a result of their fall, they have risen by a sure resurrection.

—St. John of the Ladder

428 Repentance effaces every sin when there is no delay after the fall of the soul — when the disease is not allowed to go on for a long time. For then evil will not have power to leave its mark in us, when it is drawn up at the moment it is set down, like a plant newly planted.

—St. Methodius of Olympus

429 I lost, O Lord, the use of yesterday.
Anger came and stole my heart away.
O may this morning's light until the evening stay.

—St. Gregory Nazianzen

430 O holiest Truth, how have I lied to Thee!
I vowed this day Thy festival should be.
Yet I am dim ere night.
Surely I made my prayer, and I did deem
That I could keep in me Thy morning beam
Immaculate and bright.
But my foot slipped and, as I lay, he came,

My gloomy foe, and robbed me of heaven's flame.
Help Thou my darkness, Lord, till I am light.
—St. Gregory Nazianzen

431 Repentance is an effect of faith. For unless a man believes that the object of his addiction is sin, he will not abandon it; and if he does not believe punishment is impending over the transgressor, and salvation to be the portion of him who lives according to the commandments, he will not reform.
—St. Clement of Alexandria

432 If a vessel is to be filled, it must first be empty. So cast all evil away from you, that you may be filled to the brim.
—St. Augustine

433 Helpless, I cast myself at the feet of Jesus. I watered them with my tears. I wiped them with my hair. And then I subdued my rebellious body with weeks of abstinence.
—St. Jerome

434 You will scarcely merit pardon, by turns weeping your sins and sinning.
—St. Isidore of Seville

435 Truly, my child, if I were allowed to see my sins, three or four men would not be enough to weep for them.
—Anonymous (*Sayings of the Desert Fathers*)

436 He who really keeps account of his actions considers as lost every day in which he does not mourn, no matter how much good he may have done in it.
—St. John of the Ladder

437 In everything we do and think, in everything we say, let us deny what we used to be and confess what we now are: reborn in Christ.

—St. Augustine

438 The bitter roots of fear arrest the consuming sores of our sins. Thus fear, too, is helpful, if bitter.

—St. Clement of Alexandria

439 Christ has given His priests a power He would not give to His angels, for has He not said to them, "Whatsoever you bind on earth shall be bound in heaven"?

—St. John Chrysostom

440 God has promised forgiveness to your repentance, but He has not promised tomorrow to your procrastination.

—St. Augustine

Charity

441 Like some spark lighting upon our inmost soul, love was kindled within us and burst into flame — a love for the Holy Word, the most lovely object of all, Who attracts all irresistibly toward Himself by His unutterable beauty.

—St. Gregory the Wonderworker

442 Each person is like that which he loves.

—St. Augustine

443 A man becomes God because he loves what God loves.

—St. Clement of Alexandria

444 God is love, and He is knowable to those who love Him.

—St. Clement of Alexandria

445 This is what it means to love God freely, to hope for God from God.

—St. Augustine

446 If we are able to love God it is because we have been loved by God.

—Origen

447 It is love that asks, that seeks, that knocks, that finds, and that is faithful to what it finds.

—St. Augustine

448 To none do you owe anything but to love one another.

—St. Augustine

449 One who does not love is guilty of sin.

—St. John Chrysostom

450 Love and do what you will.

—St. Augustine

451 By loving Christ we can easily bear the weaknesses of others.

—St. Augustine

452 Do you want to receive applause? Applaud another.

—St. Ambrose

453 Whatever the Christians do not wish to be done to them, they do not do to another.

—Aristides

454 The Lord does not say that the proof of His disciples' faithfulness will be the working of wondrous miracles. . . . What does He tell them? "You shall be known as my disciples if you love one another."

—St. Basil the Great

455 Let us be kind to one another after the pattern of the tender mercy and goodness of our Creator.

—Pope St. Clement I of Rome

456 Love has hands to help others. It has feet to hasten to the poor and needy. It has eyes to see misery and want. It has ears to hear the sighs and sorrows of men. This is what love looks like.

—St. Augustine

457 The love of neighbor has its bounds in each man's love of himself.

—St. Augustine

458 To harbor no envy, no anger, no resentment against an offender is still not to have charity for him. It is possible, without any charity, to avoid rendering evil for evil, because it is the law. But to render, spontaneously, good for evil — such a disposition to do good to those who hate us belongs to a perfect spiritual love.

—St. Maximus the Confessor

459 Let them say against us whatever they will. We love them even if they do not want us to.

—St. Augustine

460 Let us pray, and beg His mercy, that we may live blameless in love, free from all partiality for one man over another.

—Pope St. Clement I of Rome

461 Sympathy may not see clearly, but antipathy does not see at all.

—St. Isidore of Pelusium

462 Love is conceived in many ways: in the form of meekness, mildness, patience, liberality, freedom from envy, absence of hatred, forgetfulness of injuries. In all, it is incapable of being divided or distinguished: its nature is to communicate.

—St. Clement of Alexandria

463 Those who have the grace of charity are not content to be united in soul only; they seek for the personal presence of the one they love.

—St. John Chrysostom

464 An old man was asked, "How can I find God?" He said, "In fasting, in watching, in labors, in devotion, and, above all, in discernment. I tell you, many have injured their bodies without discernment and have gone away from us having achieved nothing. Our mouths smell bad through fasting, we know the Scriptures by heart, we recite all the Psalms of David, but we do not have what God seeks: charity and humility."

—Anonymous (*Sayings of the Desert Fathers*)

Faith

465 Nothing visible is eternal.

—St. Ignatius of Antioch

466 What is faith, except to believe what you do not see?

—St. Augustine

467 The reward of this faith is to see what we believe.

—St. Augustine

468 First a man believes, and when he believes, he loves. When he loves, he hopes. When he hopes, he is justified. When he is justified, he is perfected. When he is perfected, he is consummated. And when his whole structure is raised up, consummated, and perfected, then he becomes a house and a temple for a dwelling-place of Christ.

—St. Aphrahat

469 We can only believe if we want to.

—St. Augustine

470 I believe because it is absurd.

—Tertullian

471 If the thing believed is incredible, it is also incredible that the incredible should have been so believed.

—St. Augustine

472 Miracles do not shame all into belief, but only those of a good disposition.

—Anonymous (*Teaching of the Twelve Apostles*)

473 He does not live rightly who does not believe rightly.

—Pope St. Callistus

474 One who has no faith has no freedom of spirit.

—St. Ambrose of Milan

475 As branches dry up without the virtue of the root, so works — to whatever degree they may seem good — are nothing if they are disjoined from the solidity of the faith.

—Pope St. Gregory the Great

476 Law has not brought the Church together, but the faith of Christ.

—St. Ambrose of Milan

477 What can be hoped for but what is believed?

—St. Augustine

478 Seek not to understand that you may believe, but to believe that you may understand.

—St. Augustine

Joy

479 The Christian should be an alleluia from head to foot.

—St. Augustine

480 The perfect Christian is always a bearer of peace and joy.

—St. Clement of Alexandria

481 Beware of surrendering yourself to the tyranny of sorrow. You can command yourself; the tempest is not beyond your skill.

— St. John Chrysostom

482 Let us rejoice and give thanks, not only that we have become Christians, but that we have become Christ! Do you grasp this? Do you understand the enormous grace God has given us? Stand in awe and rejoice — we have become Christ!

—St. Augustine

483 Never be downcast. For only one thing is fearful, and that is sin.

— St. John Chrysostom

484 The Lord's prayer carries one to the higher state of prayer, to that spark-like and ineffable prayer which very few men know by experience. . . . Sometimes it happens that the soul is filled with an indescribable joy and cannot help breaking out.

—St. John Cassian

485 A feast day such as the birthday of St. Peter should be seasoned with more gladness than usual.

—St. Jerome

486 All seek joy, but it is not found on earth.

—St. John Chrysostom

487 I greet you in the blood of Jesus Christ, which is eternal and abiding joy.

—St. Ignatius of Antioch

Virtue and Vice

488 Do not be alarmed when you hear of virtue, nor feel toward the Word as if you were strangers to it. For it is not far from us; it is not external to us. The work is in us, and it is easy, if we have but the will.

—St. Anthony of Egypt

489 We need not travel for the kingdom of heaven, or cross the sea for virtue.

—St. Anthony of Egypt

490 Prize virtues and do not be the slave of glory; for the former are immortal, while the latter quickly fades.

—Anonymous (*Sayings of the Desert Fathers*)

491 It is impossible for a man to be wretched who is endowed with virtue.

—Lactantius

492 Where virtue is, there are many snares.

—St. John Chrysostom

493 A greedy appetite for food is ended by satiety, and the pleasure of drinking ends when our thirst is quenched. And so it is with the other things. . . . But the possession of virtue, once it is firmly achieved, cannot be measured by time nor limited by satiety. Rather, to those who are its disciples it appears as something ever new and fresh.

—St. Gregory of Nyssa

494 If virtue despises opulence and riches because they are frail, and pleasures because they are fleeting, it therefore despises a life that is frail and brief, that it may obtain one that is substantial and lasting.

—Lactantius

495 Of all virtues, the nature is but one and the same, although they appear to be divided into many different kinds and names: just as there is but one substance of gold, although it may seem to be distributed through many different kinds of jewelry according to the skill of the goldsmith.

—St. John Cassian

496 Virtue has need only of our will, since it is within us and springs from us. . . . If we remain as we were made, we are in the state of virtue. But if we give our minds to base things, we are accounted evil.

—St. Anthony of Egypt

497 No structure of virtue can possibly be raised in our soul unless, first, the foundations of true humility are laid in our heart.

—St. John Cassian

498 He possesses no virtue perfectly who is known to have broken down in some part of them. For how can we believe that that man has extinguished the burning heats of lust (which are kindled not only by bodily incitement but by vice of the mind), who could not quell the sharp stings of anger, which break out from intemperance of heart alone?

—St. John Cassian

499 Try to acquire the virtues you see lacking in others.

—St. Augustine

500 The soul is influenced by outward observances, and is shaped and fashioned according to its actions.

—St. Basil the Great

501 Total abstinence is easier than perfect moderation.

—St. Augustine

502 From God comes all virtue. From God come our life and our power.

—St. Cyprian of Carthage

503 The glory of fortitude does not rest only on the strength of one's body or of one's arms, but rather on the courage of the mind.

—St. Ambrose of Milan

504 Rightly is that called fortitude when a man conquers himself, restrains his anger, yields to no allurements, is not put out by misfortunes, nor gets elated by success, when he does not get carried away by every change as by some chance wind.

—St. Ambrose of Milan

505 He who chooses virtue is like one who sees all things plainly, and looks upward, who goes his way in time of clearest light. But he, on the other hand, who has involved himself in wickedness, is like a man who wanders helplessly about in a moonless night, as one who is blind, and deprived of the sight of things by his darkness.

—St. Gregory the Wonderworker

506 We make a ladder of our vices if we trample them underfoot.

—St. Augustine

507 You can tell a man's inward condition from his outward gait. By these signs, then, does carnal pride reveal itself. In conversation the man's voice is loud; in his silence there is bitterness; in his mirth his laughter is noisy and excessive; when he is serious he is unreasonably gloomy; in his answers there is rancor; he is too free with his tongue, his words tumbling out at random without being weighed. He is utterly lacking in patience, and without charity; impudent in offering insults to others; faint-hearted in bearing them himself; troublesome in the matter of obedience, except where his own wishes and likings correspond with his duty; unforgiving in receiving admonition; weak in giving up his own wishes; very stubborn about yielding to those of others; always trying to compass his own ends, and never ready to give them up for others. As a result, though he is incapable of giving sound advice, still in everything he prefers his own opinion to that of the elders.

—St. John Cassian

508 There is no vice so completely contrary to nature that it obliterates all traces of nature.

—St. Augustine

509 Some faults grow up without any natural occasion giving birth to them, but simply from the free choice of a corrupt and evil will. Envy and covetousness are caught (so to speak) from without, having no origination in us from natural instincts.

—St. John Cassian

510 The nature of gluttony is threefold: first, there is that which forces us to anticipate the proper hour for a meal, next that which delights in stuffing the stomach, and gorging all kinds of food; thirdly, that which takes pleasure in more refined and delicate feasting.

—St. John Cassian

511 Are you trying to bend the heart of God, which is always upright, so that it may fall in with the perversity of yours?

—St. Augustine

512 No duty is more urgent than that of returning thanks.

—St. Ambrose of Milan

Unity

513 There are three unions in this world: Christ and the Church, husband and wife, spirit and flesh.

—St. Augustine

514 What could be more delightful than to see all who are separated by such vast distances bound together by the union of love into one harmony of members in Christ's Body?

—St. Basil the Great

515 The same Lord Who divided the islands from the continent by the sea bound the island Christians to the continental by love. Nothing, brethren, separates us from each other but deliberate estrangement.

—St. Basil the Great

516 As this broken bread was scattered upon the mountains and, gathered together, became one, so may Your Church be gathered together from the ends of the earth into Your kingdom; for Yours is the glory and the power through Jesus Christ for ever and ever.

—Anonymous (*Teaching of the Twelve Apostles*)

517 Though scattered over the whole world, the Church diligently observes this preaching and this faith as if it occupied just one house. This it believes as if it had just one mind, and this it preaches and teaches as if it had just one mouth. And although there are many dialects in the world, the meaning of the tradition is one and the same.

—St. Irenaeus of Lyons

518 Why, then, are there strifes, tumults, divisions, schisms, and wars among you? Have we not one God and one Christ? Is there not one Spirit of grace poured out upon us? And have we not one calling in Christ? Why do we divide and tear to pieces the members of Christ, and raise up strife against our own body, and have reached such a height of madness as to forget that "we are members one of another" (Eph 4:25)?

—Pope St. Clement I of Rome

519 God does not hear those who are at enmity with their brethren in unjust quarrels, even though they should pray three times an hour.

—Anonymous (*Teaching of the Twelve Apostles*)

520 It would be monstrous to feel pleasure in the schisms and divisions of the churches, and not to consider that the greatest of goods consists in the knitting together of the members of Christ's Body.

—St. Basil the Great

521 Flee the regions where enmity, ambition, and contention have their dwelling.

—St. Ambrose of Milan

522 It is right and holy rather to obey God than to follow those who, through pride, have become the leaders of a detestable sedition. For we shall incur no slight injury, but rather great danger, if we rashly yield ourselves to the inclinations of men who aim at exciting strife and turmoil, so as to draw us away from what is good.

—Pope St. Clement I of Rome

523 You were sincere and uncorrupted, and forgetful of injuries between one another. Every kind of faction and schism was abominable in your sight. You mourned over the sins of your neighbors; their defects you called your own.

—Pope St. Clement I of Rome

524 The teacher of peace and the master of unity would not have prayer made single and individually, as for one who prays only for himself. For we do not say, "My Father, who art in heaven."

—St. Cyprian of Carthage

Obedience

525 The soul cannot proceed without someone to guide it.

—Origen

526 He is a Christian, a true Christian, who subjects himself to the rule of the one and only Word of God.

—Origen

527 Obedience is, in a way, the mother of all virtues.

—St. Augustine

528 Be obedient to your bishop and welcome him as the parent of your soul.

—St. Jerome

529 Be obedient to your bishop and to one another, as Jesus Christ in His human nature was subject to the Father and as the Apostles were to Christ and the Father. In this way there will be union of body and spirit.

—St. Ignatius of Antioch

530 Let the layman argue, and the bishop listen. Let the bishop learn of the layman. But undoubtedly, if we go through the series of the Holy Scriptures, or the times of old, who can deny that, in a matter of faith — in a matter, I say, of faith — bishops are accustomed to judge of Christian emperors, not emperors of bishops?

—St. Ambrose of Milan

531 Obedience is a greater virtue than chastity, however perfect. Chastity carries within it the danger of pride, but obedience has within it the promise of humility.

—Anonymous (*Sayings of the Desert Fathers*)

Integrity and Constancy

532 To be sound in faith and holy in life — this is the kernel of Christianity.

—St. Augustine

533 To be a Christian — not merely to seem one — is the great thing.

—St. Jerome

534 Poison wears the beauty of lilies; and though their buds may conceal it and disguise it, it blossoms in their bitter flowers.

—St. Ephrem of Syria

535 The person who is dedicated to Christ is equally earnest in small things as in great.

—St. Jerome

536 Words would be superfluous if we had deeds to show for them.

—St. John Chrysostom

537 To speak well belongs only to a few, but to live well belongs to all.

—Lactantius

538 In the evening we exalted Him; in the morning we rejected Him. When necessity left us, faithfulness left us.

—St. Ephrem of Syria

539 No one can harm the man who does himself no wrong.

—St. John Chrysostom

540 Be true to yourself, and no one can harm you.
—St. John Chrysostom

541 Nothing artificial is really pleasing.
—St. Ambrose of Milan

542 When the old man [Abbot John] was readily going to depart to his own, was lying at his last gasp, and the brethren were standing round, they implored and begged that he would leave them, as a sort of legacy, some special charge by which they could attain to the height of perfection, the more easily from the brevity of the charge: he sighed and said, "I never did my own will, nor taught any one what I had not first done myself."
—St. John Cassian

543 O the miserable state of waverers! With what seas of cares, with what storms they are tossed! For now at one time, as the wind drives them, they are carried away headlong into error. At another time, coming again to themselves, they are beaten back like contrary waves.
—St. Vincent of Lerins

544 With your honorable conduct and your irreproachable deeds, prepare the Lord's way, smooth out his path so that the Word of God may act in you without hindrance and give you the knowledge of His mysteries and of His coming.

—Origen

Patience and Peace

545 Peace is our final good.

—St. Augustine

546 It is a noble achievement for a Christian to have no disputes with anyone. But if by any circumstance or temptation, a dispute arises, let him try to remain composed, even if this means losing.

—Anonymous (*Teaching of the Twelve Apostles*)

547 Here, we are happy when we have peace, such little peace as can be had in a good life; but that happiness, in comparison with our final happiness, is altogether misery.

—St. Augustine

548 Where there is anger, there the Lord is not. For that anger which is the friend of Satan — anger that is aroused unjustly by false brethren — never advances the unanimity of the Church.

—Anonymous (*Teaching of the Twelve Apostles*)

549 If we are enjoined to love our enemies, whom have we to hate?

—Tertullian

550 If injured, we are forbidden to retaliate, lest we become as bad ourselves. Who can suffer injury at our hands?

—Tertullian

551 What I need is the meekness by which the prince of this world is destroyed.

—St. Ignatius of Antioch

552 When the aged John, who was superior of a large monastery and of a number of brethren, had come to visit the aged Paesius, who was living in a vast desert, and had been asked of him as of a very old friend, what he had done in all the forty years in which he had been separated from him and had scarcely ever been disturbed in his solitude by the brethren: "Never," said he, "has the sun seen me eating," "nor me angry," said the other.

—St. John Cassian

553 Hope is patience with the lamp lit.

—Tertullian

554 You touched me, and I burned for Your peace.

—St. Augustine

Forgiveness

555 Mercy imitates God and disappoints Satan.

—St. John Chrysostom

556 If you have anything against anyone, forgive it. You come here to receive forgiveness of sins, and you, too, must forgive him who has sinned against you. Or how will you say to the Lord, "Forgive me my many sins," if you have not yourself forgiven your fellow-servant even his little sins.

—St. Cyril of Jerusalem

557 As good parents do, you have readily granted pardon after being asked. Had you forgiven before being asked, it would have been not forgiveness but approval of their conduct.

—St. Ambrose of Milan

558 If you have forgiven your brother four hundred and ninety times, you should still multiply your acts of gentleness, to do good for your own sake. Although he does not do so yet, still you should try to forgive your brother for God's sake . . . that when you pray, you may be heard as a friend of God.

—Anonymous (*Teaching of the Twelve Apostles*)

559 An insult is either sustained or destroyed — not by the disposition of those who insult, but by the disposition of those who bear it.

—St. John Chrysostom

560 He has pardoned us and we have not pardoned. . . . The guilt we commit we write anew. "Pardon, O Lord," we cry. "Avenge, O Lord," we pray. "Pardon," indeed, when we have done wrong; "avenge," indeed, when we are wronged.

—St. Ephrem of Syria

561 If you do not receive him who repents, because you are merciless, you sin against the Lord God; for you do not obey Our Lord and God in acting as He acted.

—Anonymous (*Teaching of the Twelve Apostles*)

Humility

562 If you ask me what is the first thing in religion, I will reply that the first, second, and third thing is humility.
—St. Augustine

563 Imitate the ass in his love for his master.
—St. John Chrysostom

564 Do not seek to confer any greater favor upon me than that I be sacrificed to God.
—St. Ignatius of Antioch

565 Arrogance and boldness belong to those who are accursed of God.
—Pope St. Clement I of Rome

566 The desire for fame tempts even noble minds.
—St. Augustine

567 Man is often vain about his contempt of glory.
—St. Augustine

568 Behave as if you were a stranger and, wherever you are, do not expect your words to have an influence, and you will be at peace.
—Anonymous (*Sayings of the Desert Fathers*)

569 It is not true humility if a man, perceiving that it is God's will that he should rank above others, refuses to do so.
—Pope St. Gregory the Great

570 Neither asceticism, nor vigils, nor any kind of suffering are able to save. Only true humility can do that.

—Anonymous (*Sayings of the Desert Fathers*)

571 There is something in humility that strangely exalts the heart.

—St. Augustine

572 After the royal throne comes death; after the dunghill comes the kingdom of heaven.

—St. John Chrysostom

573 Even if an angel should indeed appear to you, do not receive him but humiliate yourself, saying, "I am not worthy to see an angel, for I am a sinner."

—Anonymous (*Sayings of the Desert Fathers*)

574 This is the mark of Christianity — however much a man works, and however many righteous deeds he performs, to feel that he has done nothing, and in fasting to say, "This is not fasting," and in praying, "This is not prayer," and in perseverance at prayer, "I have shown no perseverance; I am only just beginning to practice and to struggle"; and even if he is righteous before God, he should say, "I am not righteous, not I; I do not struggle, but only make a beginning every day."

—St. Macarius

575 I saw the snares that the enemy spreads out over the world and I said groaning, "What can get through from such snares?" Then I heard a voice saying to me, "Humility."

—St. Anthony the Great

576 Do not become swollen-headed if you have served well, because you have only done what you were supposed to do.

—St. Ambrose of Milan

577 How shall we acquire saving humility, abandoning the deadly elevation of pride? By practicing some act of humility in everything we do.

—St. Basil the Great

578 Follow after humility, as one in love with it. Be in love with it, and it shall glorify you.

—St. Basil the Great

579 What are the honors of this world but puff and emptiness and danger of falling?

—St. Augustine

580 Familiarity wastes away admiration.

—St. John Chrysostom

581 The proud one does not know himself. If he knew himself and his own stupidity, he would not be conceited.

—St. Mark the Hermit

582 One cannot reach the goal of perfection and purity except through true humility, displayed first of all to one's brothers, and shown also to God in one's inmost heart. For without His protection and aid extended at every instant, he cannot obtain the perfection he desires.

—St. John Cassian

583 It is folly to undertake a hard and difficult task just to be admired, to put great effort into keeping God's commandments with only an earthly reward in mind.

—Pope St. Gregory the Great

584 The power that makes men terrible is a terror first to its possessors. It smiles and frowns; it flatters and deceives; it lifts up and casts down.

—St. Cyprian of Carthage

585 What can be more noble than to train your mind not to place a high value on riches, pleasures, and honors, nor to waste all your care on these?

—St. Ambrose of Milan

586 To pass life in hiding I count among the highest goods.

—St. Basil the Great

Chastity and Purity

587 Chastity has three forms: one that of married life, a second that of widowhood, and a third that of virginity. We do not extol one to the exclusion of others.

—St. Ambrose of Milan

588 If we offer to Him our chastity, that is, our body's chastity, we receive from Him chastity of the spirit.

—Origen

589 Praise and hatred and love based on physical beauty belong to unchaste souls. Seek instead for beauty of soul.

—St. John Chrysostom

590 He has no lasting purity and chastity who is not contented always to keep to a well-balanced and temperate diet.

—St. John Cassian

591 He then will never be able to check the motions of a burning lust who cannot restrain the desires of the appetite.

—St. John Cassian

592 Lust is an appetite of the mind by which temporal goods are preferred to eternal goods.

—St. Augustine

593 It is not good to look at what it is not lawful to desire.

—Pope St. Gregory the Great

594 An unchaste eye is the messenger of an unchaste heart.

—St. Augustine

595 Chastity will be lost where the distinction between the sexes is not observed.

—St. Ambrose

596 Purity of soul cannot be lost without consent.

—St. Augustine

597 Modesty is praised in humans because it is not a matter of nature, but of will.

—Lactantius

598 It is better to marry only because it is worse to burn. It is still better neither to marry nor to burn.

—Tertullian

Conversation

599 I ask God — Who supplies both the speaking and the hearing to us — that I may speak so that you may be made better by hearing, and that you may listen so that I, the speaker, may not be disappointed.

—Anonymous (*Letter to Diognetus*)

600 It is a good thing to use the tongue sparingly, and to keep a calm and rightly balanced heart in the use of speech. For it is not right to say things that are foolish and absurd, or to utter all that occurs to the mind. We ought instead to know and reflect that, though we are far separated from heaven, God hears what we say, and that it is good for us to speak without offense.

—St. Gregory the Wonderworker

601 Know how to converse — to interrogate without over-earnestness; to answer without desire of display; not to interrupt a profitable speaker, nor to desire ambitiously to put in a word of one's own; to be measured in speaking and hearing; not to be ashamed of receiving information, or to be grudging in giving it; nor to disown what one has learned from others. . . . One should reflect first what one is going to say and then say it. Be courteous when addressed, amiable in social exchanges; not aiming to be pleasant by smartness, but cultivating gentleness in kind admonitions. Harshness is ever to be put aside, even in censuring.

—St. Basil the Great

602 Anything pleasant easily persuades, and while it gives pleasure it fixes itself in the heart.

—Lactantius

603 Hear the other side.

—St. Augustine

604 We must learn to arrange very cautiously a proper time, and when the voice is to open the mouth prudently, and also to arrange wisely the time when silence is to close it.

—Pope St. Gregory the Great

605 He who sees any evil in his neighbor and keeps silent about it acts like the surgeon who looks at his friend's wound and will not cure it.

—Pope St. Gregory the Great

606 An arrow never lodges in a stone: often it recoils upon the bowman. Let the detractor learn, from your unwillingness to listen, not to be so eager to detract.

—St. Jerome

607 There is a plentiful multitude of words, but there is no profit from random and foolish talking.

—St. Gregory the Wonderworker

608 The human race is naturally insatiable in its thirst for speaking and hearing. It is man's habit, too, to want to lay his idle eyes upon all that happens. Yet what can occur or what can be done by men that has not been done already? What new thing is there worthy of mention?

—St. Gregory the Wonderworker

609 There are many men who, not wishing to be thought fools, often try to speak more than is profitable for them to do, and they are led astray in their meditation.

—Pope St. Gregory the Great

Correction

610 If an offense comes out of the truth, it is better that the offense come than that the truth be concealed.

—St. Jerome

611 To arraign sinners is to admonish those in a like state, and to praise the virtuous is to quicken the zeal of those who wish to do right.

—St. Jerome

612 I count it greater to be reproved than to reprove, since it is more excellent to free oneself from evil than to free another.

—St. Methodius of Olympus

613 Diseased flesh calls for the scalpel. . . . With a cruelty that is really kindness, a physician, in order to spare, does not spare, and in order to be merciful, is cruel.

—St. Jerome

614 It will be good of you to take this castigation well. If you do not, I will give you more of it.

—St. Gregory of Nazianzen

615 Christians free men from serpents when they uproot evil from their hearts by exhorting them to do good.

—Pope St. Gregory the Great

616 The ax of the Gospel must be now laid to the root of the barren tree, and both it and its fruitless foliage cast into the fire.

—St. Jerome

617 Rebukes are often better than silent friendship.

— St. Ambrose of Milan

618 Correct one another, not in anger, but in composure, as you read in the Gospel.

—Anonymous (*Teaching of the Twelve Apostles*)

Teaching and Learning

619 Let us learn upon earth the knowledge that will continue with us in heaven.

—St. Jerome

620 Study as if you were to live forever. Live as if you were to die tomorrow.

—St. Isidore of Seville

621 Many who were never disciples wish to be teachers, and they think the burden of teaching very light, because they do not know the power of its greatness.

—Pope St. Gregory the Great

622 The seed of words grows very well when the humanity of the teacher softens and moistens the breast of the hearer.

—Pope St. Gregory the Great

623 It is a wonderful thing for an upright man who cannot teach others by precept to teach them by the piety of his conduct.

—Cassiodorus

624 It is not by nature, but by learning, that people become noble and good, as people also become physicians and pilots.

—St. Clement of Alexandria

625 A man can be a believer without learning, but it is impossible for a man without learning to comprehend the things declared in the faith.

—St. Clement of Alexandria

626 How excellent might my life be, if I were but a listener to the addresses of my teacher, and silent myself!

—St. Gregory the Wonderworker

627 Words are the progeny of the soul. Hence we call those who have instructed us "fathers."

—St. Clement of Alexandria

628 Christ has appointed us to be like lamps, so as to be teachers to others.

—St. John Chrysostom

629 Do not give your ear to every man, lest liars overwhelm you. Do not lend your foot to every man, lest vile ones misguide you. Do not give your soul to every man, lest the insolent trample you. Keep your hand from the false man, lest he gather thorns into your hand.

—St. Ephrem of Syria

630 Whoever follows after what is inferior to himself, becomes himself inferior.

—St. Augustine

631 One thing especially, child of God, will I admonish you: to possess your mind with a love of sacred reading.

—St. Jerome

632 Through reading you perceive one of two things — either what you can desire or what you can endure.

—Cassiodorus

Wisdom and Truth

633 There is no more pleasant food for the soul than the knowledge of truth.

—Lactantius

634 Wisdom — that is, the inquiry after truth — is natural to all.

—Lactantius

635 All, in my opinion, are illuminated by the dawn of Light. Let all, therefore — both Greeks and barbarians — all who have aspired after the truth — both those who possess much, and those who have any portion — produce whatever they have of the word of truth.

—St. Clement of Alexandria

636 Where, then, is wisdom? It consists in thinking neither that you know all things, which is the property of God; nor that you are ignorant of all things, which is the way of a beast. Man's place is, rather, somewhere in the middle.

—Lactantius

637 If your thought is without any alloy of evil, free from passion, and alien from stain, you are blessed because you are clear of sight.

—St. Gregory of Nyssa

638 Your head is clear and all your senses keen. If you were to add to this wisdom and eloquence a careful study and knowledge of Scripture, I should soon see you defending our citadel against all attackers.

—St. Jerome

639 I have said to wisdom, "You are my sister." With this I bridle my impetuous anger, with this I appease wasting envy, with this I lull to rest sorrow, the chain of the heart; with this I sober the flood of pleasure, with this I put a measure not on friendship, but on dislike.

—St. Gregory Nazianzen

640 Patience is the companion to wisdom.

—St. Augustine

641 I would deem a small and sparsely populated city to be great and powerful if it had but one wise man, however poor, among its citizens.

—St. Gregory the Wonderworker

642 Pardon may be granted to those who are ignorant and do not call themselves wise; but it cannot be extended to those who, while professing wisdom, show themselves to be foolish.

—Lactantius

643 The rude and simple brother must not suppose himself a saint just because he knows nothing; and he who is educated and eloquent must not measure his saintliness merely by his fluency. Of two imperfect things, holy rusticity is better than sinful eloquence.

—St. Jerome

644 The common people have sometimes more wisdom, because they are only as wise as is necessary. And if you ask them whether they know anything or nothing, they will say that they know the things they know, and will confess that they are ignorant of what they are ignorant.

—Lactantius

645 Religion should not be undertaken without wisdom, nor any wisdom approved without religion.

—Lactantius

646 Apart from knowledge of his Creator, every man is but a brute.

—St. Jerome

647 Truth is the property of God, before whom I wish to be entirely blameless.

—Synesius of Cyrene

648 To understand what is false is truly part of wisdom, but of *human* wisdom. Beyond this, man cannot proceed. . . . But to know the truth is the part of divine wisdom. Yet man by himself cannot achieve this knowledge unless he is taught by God. Thus, philosophers have reached the height of human wisdom, just to understand what is not; but they have failed to achieve the power of saying what really is.

—Lactantius

649 Many philosophers discussed the nature of good and evil, yet from the compulsion of nature lived in a manner different from their discourse, because they were without virtue. Virtue united with knowledge is wisdom.

—Lactantius

650 I failed to see the light with my blinded eyes; but I attributed the fault not to them, but to the sun.

—St. Jerome

651 The truth still lies hidden in obscurity — either through the error and ignorance of the common people, who are the slaves of various and foolish superstitions, or through the philosophers, who by the perversity of their minds confuse rather than throw light upon it.

—Lactantius

652 Truth knows that she is a stranger on earth and easily finds enemies among men of another allegiance. But she knows that her race, home, hope, recompense, honor are in heaven.

—Tertullian

653 There is some perverse power that is always hostile to the truth, that rejoices in the errors of men, whose one and only task is perpetually to scatter darkness and blind the minds of men, lest they should see the light — lest, in short, they should look to heaven.

—Lactantius

654 This is the cause of their perversity — ignorance of themselves. And if anyone, after gaining the knowledge of truth, should shake off this ignorance, he will know to what end his life should be directed, and how it should be spent.

—Lactantius

655 Those who without judgment approve the discoveries of their ancestors are without wisdom, led like sheep by others.

—Lactantius

656 If wisdom follows knowledge, so troubles attend on wisdom.

—St. Gregory the Wonderworker

657 Simple and undisguised truth should be more clear, because it has sufficient ornament of itself. It is corrupted when embellished with ornaments.

—Lactantius

658 The power of truth is so great that it defends itself, even in small things, by its own clarity.

—Lactantius

659 Wisdom, unless it is engaged on some action on which it may exert its force, is empty and false.

—Lactantius

660 We glorify God, Who has given you the grace not only to have the right opinions, but also, so far as is possible, not to be ignorant of the devices of the devil.

—St. Athanasius

661 Accept humbly what God has revealed to us. Don't try to probe what God has kept hidden.

—St. John Chrysostom

662 Nothing is more excellent than knowledge.

—St. John of Damascus

663 Our knowledge is Christ; our wisdom is again the same Christ. . . . By means of Him we tend toward Him. By means of knowledge we tend toward wisdom, all the same without departing from one and the same Christ.

—St. Augustine

664 Even if the entire human race were submerged in sleep, it would still be true that three times three equals nine.

—St. Augustine

665 What contradicts truth cannot be just.

—St. Augustine

Doctrine

666 Be a lamp in brightness, and make the works of darkness cease, so that whenever your doctrine shines, no man may dare to heed the desires of darkness.

—St. Ephrem of Syria

667 Content with the provision that God had made for you, and carefully attending to His Words, you were inwardly filled with His doctrine, and His sufferings were before your eyes.

—Pope St. Clement I of Rome

668 Thus do we teach, thus do we preach. These are the apostolic doctrines of the Church, for which we would die.

—St. Alexander of Alexandria

669 Though the truth may be defended without eloquence — and it often is — still it needs to be explained and discussed with distinctness and elegance of speech, in order that it may flow with greater power into the minds of men.

—Lactantius

670 It often happens that when it becomes necessary to defend certain points of Catholic doctrine against the insidious attacks of heresy, they are more carefully studied, they become more clearly understood, they are more earnestly inculcated, and so the very questions raised by heretics give occasion to a more thorough knowledge of the subject in question.

—St. Augustine

671 We must not, even in a trivial matter, turn aside from the path of truth.

—St. Epiphanius

672 I will have no deceit about dogmas, nor shall there be variance between my thoughts and my tongue.

—Synesius of Cyrene

673 No one can call it intrusion if, with a most affectionate interest, we are eager to warn you against doctrines contrary to the grace of God.

—St. Jerome

674 All doctrine must be prejudged as false if it appears to contradict the truth of the churches and Apostles of Christ and God.

—Tertullian

675 It is human to err; it is devilish to remain in error.

—St. Augustine

676 Not only in the exercise of virtue and the keeping of the commandments, but also in the path of faith, the way that leads to life is narrow and difficult. It requires great pains, and involves great risks, to walk without stumbling along the one footway of sound doctrine, amid the uncertain opinions and the plausible untruths of the unskillful, and to escape all peril of mistake when the toils of error are on every side.

—Pope St. Leo the Great

677 He who has fallen into heresy passes through an arid wilderness, abandoning the only true God, destitute of God, seeking waterless water, reaching an uninhabited and thirsty land, collecting sterility with his hands.

—St. Clement of Alexandria

678 What we see before us is no mere bodily slavery, but a carrying away of souls into captivity, perpetrated day by day by the champions of heresy. If you are not, even now, moved to console us, before long all will have fallen under the dominion of the heresy, and you will find none left to whom you may hold out your hand.

—St. Basil the Great

679 Send to the bishops of the West, from your holy Church, men powerful in sound doctrine. Tell them of our present calamities. Suggest to them the mode of relieving us.

—St. Basil the Great

680 Peace I desire if orthodoxy goes with it; but peace I reject if it is unrighteous and heterodox.

—Theodoret of Cyrrhus

681 The truth is warped when some teach one set of dogmas, others another.

—St. Clement of Alexandria

682 In necessary things, unity; in doubtful things, liberty; in all things, charity.

—St. Augustine

683 I was unable to express in writing even what I seemed to understand; and whatever I wrote was unequal to the imperfect shadow of truth that was in my mind . . . I frequently planned to stop writing; believe me, I did. But lest I should disappoint you, or lest my silence should lead into impiety those contentious people who have made enquiry of you, I constrained myself to write.

—St. Athanasius

Silence

684 The brethren who were assembled said to Abba Pambo, "Say something to the Archbishop, so that he may be edified." The old man said to them, "If he is not edified by my silence, he will not be edified by my speech."

—Anonymous (*Sayings of the Desert Fathers*)

685 Silence is indeed the friend and helpmate of thought and invention.

—St. Gregory the Wonderworker

686 If you do not find peace, why do you speak? Be silent, and when a conversation takes place, prefer to listen rather than talk.

—Anonymous (*Sayings of the Desert Fathers*)

687 A properly kept silence is a beautiful thing. It is nothing less than the father of very wise thoughts.

—Diodicus

688 To understand You, we must be silent. And for fallible conjecture to trace You even vaguely, nothing must even be whispered.

—Arnobius

689 Though I have left the city's haunts, as the source of innumerable ills, yet I have not yet learned to leave myself.

—St. Basil the Great

690 We must strive after a quiet mind.

—St. Basil the Great

691 If you give me a quiet hearing, I will tell you the mystery of simplicity.

—Anonymous (*Scillitan Acts of Martyrdom*)

692 Solitude . . . stills our passions and gives our reason an opportunity to cut them out of the soul.

—St. Basil the Great

693 I am trying to be hidden, and I embrace quiet before anything else.

—Theodoret of Cyrrhus

694 Quiet is the first step in our sanctification; the tongue purified from the gossip of the world; the eyes unexcited by fair color or comely shape; the ear not relaxing the tone of the mind by voluptuous songs, nor by that special mischief, the talk of comedians and clowns.

—St. Basil the Great

695 Give me peace and quiet above all things.

—St. Gregory Nazianzen

696 The mind, saved from dissipation from without . . . falls back upon itself and thereby ascends to the contemplation of God.

—St. Basil the Great

697 It is better for a man to be silent and be [a Christian], than to talk and not to be one. It is good to teach, if he who speaks also acts.

—St. Ignatius of Antioch

698 Not only for every idle word, but for every idle silence shall we be called to account.

—St. Ambrose of Milan

699 Never incline your ear to words of mischief. . . . Led by our sinful nature, we readily favor those who flatter us; and although we reply that we are unworthy, and a warm blush suffuses our cheeks, we readily favor those who flatter us.

—St. Jerome

700 You ask what my silence means? It means measurement of speaking, and not speaking. For he who can do it in whole, will more easily do it in part.

—St. Gregory Nazianzen

701 To hear what is fitting is not less precious than to speak it.

—St. Gregory Nazianzen

702 Just as, from standing perpetually open, the door of the bath lets all the heat out from within, so, too, when the soul yields to a wish to talk a lot, even when everything it says is good, it dissipates its recollection through the door of its voice.

—Diodicus

703 Let all mortal flesh keep silence, and stand with fear and trembling, and meditate nothing earthly within itself. For the King of kings and Lord of lords, Christ our God, comes forward to be sacrificed, and to be given for food to the faithful.

—Liturgy of St. James

Work

704 To labor is to pray.

—St. Benedict of Nursia

705 By minding your own trade and employment, try to do what is acceptable to God.

—Anonymous (*Teaching of the Twelve Apostles*)

706 Since we are convinced that God is to be found everywhere, we plow our fields praising the Lord, we sail the seas and ply all our other trades singing His mercies.

—St. Clement of Alexandria

707 Good works should be the daily nourishment of your hearts. Your bodies are fed with food and your spirits with good works.

—Pope St. Gregory the Great

708 Strength of mind and of body grows slack without the exercise of labor.

—Minucius Felix

709 Work is a powerful medicine.

—St. John Chrysostom

710 Where our work is, there let our joy be.

—Tertullian

711 Now is the time for glory and for much gain. The merchant does not get together his cargo by sitting down in harbor, but by venturing across the open seas.

— St. John Chrysostom

712 There was in the cells an old man called Apollo. If someone came to find him doing a piece of work, he would set out joyfully, saying, "I am going to work with Christ today, for the salvation of my soul, for that is the reward He gives."

—Anonymous (*Sayings of the Desert Fathers*)

713 There is no labor where one loves — or, if there is, the labor itself is loved.

—St. Augustine

714 The strivings of lovers are not burdensome. . . . When one is in love, either he does not feel the burden or he loves to feel it.

—St. Augustine

715 The bee is more honored than other animals, not because she labors, but because she labors for others.

—St. John Chrysostom

716 So you wanted to live a quiet life? But God wanted otherwise.

—St. Augustine

717 Lord, if I am still necessary to Your people, I do not decline the labor. Your will be done.

—St. Martin of Tours

718 How can God — Who is a spirit and Who cannot be

touched — be sought with hands in any other sense than by good works.

—St. Augustine

719 Idleness is the enemy of the soul.

—St. Benedict of Nursia

720 The Lord our God hates the slothful. None of those who are dedicated to God ought to be idle.

—Anonymous (*Teaching of the Twelve Apostles*)

721 Idleness is the mother of famine.

—Anonymous (*Teaching of the Twelve Apostles*)

722 Do not be a shiftless man who roams about the streets, without just cause, to spy out those who live wickedly.

—Anonymous (*Teaching of the Twelve Apostles*)

723 See that no restless brother is by chance idle or chattering and not intent on his reading and so of no profit to himself and a distraction to others.

—St. Benedict of Nursia

724 At the present time, there are many words among men, but we need works.

—Anonymous (*Sayings of the Desert Fathers*)

725 Show forth all good and holy things by deeds more than by words.

—St. Benedict of Nursia

726 In the matter of piety, poverty serves us better than wealth, and work better than idleness.

—St. John Chrysostom

727 The chief of your good works is this: that you know God, and serve Him.

—St. Melito of Sardis

728 Do what you can do, and pray for what you cannot yet do.

—St. Augustine

729 Wells, when pumped, yield purer water; and the well from which no one draws turns putrid. Use keeps steel brighter, but disuse makes it rust. In a word, exercise produces a healthy condition both in souls and bodies.

—St. Clement of Alexandria

730 I am not content with mediocrity for you: I desire all that you do to be of the highest excellence.

—St. Jerome

Friendship

731 Let us show a friend our heart, and he will open his to us. . . . A friend, if he is true, hides nothing.

—St. Ambrose of Milan

732 There is no greater invitation to love than loving first.

—St. Augustine

733 Let them know us as comforters in sorrow rather than as guests in time of mirth.

—St. Jerome

734 Among our most notorious adversaries are people destined to be our friends.

—St. Augustine

735 Come to me and revive my virtue, and work with me; and whatever benefit we once gained together, preserve for me by your prayers, lest otherwise I fade away little by little, like a shadow when the day declines. For you are my breath, more than the air, and so far only do I live as I am in your company, either present or, if absent, by your image.

—St. Gregory of Nazianzen

736 Rightly has a friend been called "the half of my soul."

—St. Augustine

737 There is no true friendship unless you weld it between souls that cleave together through the charity shed in our hearts by the Holy Spirit.

—St. Augustine

738 Here is how a friend differs from a flatterer: the flatterer speaks to give pleasure, but the friend refrains from nothing, even that which gives pain.

—St. Basil the Great

739 True friendship should never conceal what it thinks.

—St. Jerome

740 True friendship can harbor no suspicion; a friend must speak to his friend as freely as to his second self.

—St. Jerome

741 It is not a light effort, but it demands an energetic soul and a great mind to bear separation from one whom we love in the charity of Christ.

—St. John Chrysostom

Marriage and Family

742 Marriage is more than human; it is a miniature kingdom, which is the little house of the Lord.
—St. Clement of Alexandria

743 Nothing so welds our life together as the love of man and wife. For this, many will lay aside even their arms; for this they will give up life itself.
—St. John Chrysostom

744 Our Savior went to the wedding feast to make holy the origins of human life.
—St. Clement of Alexandria

745 Who are the "two or three gathered" in the name of Christ, in whose midst is the Lord? Aren't they man, wife, and child — because man and wife are joined by God?
—St. Clement of Alexandria

746 How shall we ever be able adequately to describe marriage, which the Church arranges, the Sacrifice strengthens, upon which the blessing sets a seal, at which angels are present as witnesses, and to which the Father gives His consent?
—Tertullian

747 An intelligent, discreet, and pious young woman is worth more than all the money in the world. Tell her that you love her more than your own life, because this present life is nothing, and that your only hope is that the two of you pass through this life in such a way that, in the world to come, you will be united in perfect love.

—St. John Chrysostom

748 How beautiful the marriage of two Christians, two who are one in hope, one in desire, one in the way of life they follow, one in the religion they practice.

—Tertullian

749 If you truly love your children, if you show them the full and paternal sweetness of love, you ought to be the more charitable, that by your righteous works you may commend your children to God.

—St. Cyprian of Carthage

750 You will find among us men and women growing old unmarried in the hope of living in closer communion with God.

—Athenagoras of Athens

751 Christ Himself, although in the flesh a virgin, was in the spirit a monogamist, having one wife, the Church.

—St. Jerome

752 By the counsels of holy men, states are managed well, and the household too.

—St. Clement of Alexandria

753 Marriage, as a sacred image, must be kept pure from those things that defile it. We should rise from our slumbers with the Lord, and retire to sleep with thanksgiving and prayer.

—St. Clement of Alexandria

754 The hearts of lovers have wings. . . . Love can turn to hate if there creep in too many reasons for disrespect.
—St. Clement of Alexandria

755 He who seeks only sexual pleasure turns his marriage into fornication.
—St. Clement of Alexandria

756 Birth control is premature murder. It makes no difference whether it is a life already born that one snatches away or a life that is coming to birth.
—Tertullian

757 Intercourse with even a lawful spouse is unlawful and wicked if the conception of offspring is prevented.
—St. Augustine

758 The glory of fathers is the holiness of their children.
—Anonymous (*Teaching of the Twelve Apostles*)

Poverty and Riches

759 Seek what suffices, seek what is enough, and don't desire more. Whatever goes beyond that produces anxiety, not relief.

—St. Augustine

760 You said it well — "I have nothing" — not because you lack what another has, but because you think that things will make you happy.

—St. John Chrysostom

761 For love of that true life, think of yourself — even in this world — as desolate, whatever be your outward prosperity.

—St. Augustine

762 Though many of us are called poor, this is not our disgrace, but our glory; for as our mind is relaxed by luxury, so it is strengthened by frugality.

—Minucius Felix

763 Who can be poor if he does not desire, if he does not crave for the possessions of others, if he is rich towards God?

—Minucius Felix

764 He is poor, who, although he has much, desires more.

—Minucius Felix

765 He who has nothing to lose — except these poor

garments and a few books — runs no risk of confisca-
tion.

—St. Basil the Great

766 No one can be so poor as he is born.

—Minucius Felix

767 He who walks a road is happier the lighter he walks.
So happier is he, in this journey of life, who lifts himself
along in poverty, and does not breathe heavily under the
burden of riches.

—Minucius Felix

768 I read the Gospel, and I saw that a great means of
reaching perfection was to sell one's goods, share them
with the poor, giving up of all care for this life and refus-
ing to allow the soul to be turned by any sympathy to
things of earth.

—St. Basil the Great

769 Almsgiving requires money, but even this shines
with a brighter luster when the alms are given from our
poverty. The widow who paid the two pennies was poorer
than any human, but she outdid them all.

—St. John Chrysostom

770 Widows and orphans are to be revered like the altar.

—Anonymous (*Teaching of the Twelve Apostles*)

771 If everyone took only what he needed and gave the
rest to those in need, there would be no such thing as rich
or poor.

—St. Basil the Great

772 The rich do not reap as much pleasure from what is present as they endure sorrow for what has not yet been added.

—St. John Chrysostom

773 What can be more pitiful than this rich man whose daily prayer is that there may be famine so that he may have a little gold?

—St. John Chrysostom

774 It is absurd and disgraceful for one to live magnificently and luxuriously when so many go hungry.

—St. Clement of Alexandria

775 From prosperity arises luxury; and from luxury, together with all other vices, there arises impiety towards God.

—Lactantius

776 We should not throw away things that can benefit our neighbor. Goods are called good because they can be used for good. They are instruments of good in the hands of those who use them properly.

—St. Clement of Alexandria

777 Plenty ever breeds contempt.

—Tertullian

778 Riches are not forbidden, but the pride of them is.

—St. John Chrysostom

779 What good is it to acquire what we cannot carry away with us? Far different are prudence, justice, temperance, fortitude, understanding, charity, love of the poor, faith toward Christ, gentleness, hospitality. If we obtain these, we shall find that they have preceded us and have made ready a dwelling for us in the country of the meek.

—St. Anthony of Egypt

780 The rich man is not one who possesses much, but one who gives much.

—St. John Chrysostom

781 Nothing that is God's is obtainable by money.

—Tertullian

782 What God wants is not golden chalices, but golden souls.

—St. John Chrysostom

783 He does not see, poor wretch, that his life is but a gilded torture, that he is bound fast by his wealth, and that his money owns him rather than he owns it.

—St. Ambrose of Milan

784 Nothing is more fallacious than wealth. Today it is for you; tomorrow it is against you. . . . It is a hostile comrade, a domestic enemy.

—St. John Chrysostom

785 A man who receives something from another because of his poverty or his need has therein his reward, and because he is ashamed, when he repays it he does so in secret. But it is the opposite for the Lord God; he receives in secret, but he repays in the presence of the angels, the archangels, and the righteous.

—Anonymous (*Sayings of the Desert Fathers*)

786 As if they were blind, men seeking God stumbled upon stones and blocks of wood; and those who were rich stumbled upon gold and silver, and were kept by their stumblings from finding what they were looking for.

—St. Melito of Sardis

787 The poor man, even if he is a slave and unable to fill his belly, at least enjoys the refreshment of sleep; but the lust of riches brings on sleepless nights and anxieties of mind.

—St. Gregory the Wonderworker

788 Ambitious men are ever spending, on self-indulgence and bribery, possessions that they hold in trust for the poor.

—St. Basil the Great

789 Gold does not allow men to be men, but wild beasts and fiends.

—St. John Chrysostom

790 It is impossible, in this small space, to list all those Scriptures that declare not just robbery horrible, but also the grasping mind, and the tendency to meddle with what belongs to others.

—St. Gregory the Wonderworker

791 The beauty of your mind and the brilliance of chaste speech are asked of you; the brightness of faith, not the tinkling of silver.

—St. Ambrose of Milan

Giving

792 Feeding the hungry is a greater work than raising the dead.

—St. John Chrysostom

793 Give something, however small, to the one in need. For it is not small to one who has nothing. Neither is it small to God, if we have given what we could.

—St. Gregory Nazianzen

794 Find out how much God has given you and take from it what you need; the remainder, which you do not require, is needed by others.

—St. John Chrysostom

795 See those Christians, how they love one another.

—Tertullian

796 We who are united in heart and soul have no hesitation in sharing things.

—Tertullian

797 Your burden will be lightened if you give away some of your load, and what remains will be no burden.

—St. Ambrose of Milan

798 Tithes ought to be paid, whatever your occupation. He who has given us the whole has thought it right to ask a tenth. It is not for His benefit, but for ours.

—St. Augustine

799 If you do not give the tenth part to God, He will take the nine parts.

—St. Ambrose of Milan

800 It is right to supply want, but it is not well to support laziness.

—St. Clement of Alexandria

801 The bread that you store up belongs to the hungry. The cloak that lies in your chest belongs to the naked. And the gold that you have hidden in the ground belongs to the poor.

—St. Basil the Great

802 While your dog is stuffed with food, Christ is weak with hunger.

—St. John Chrysostom

803 The best almsgiver is one who keeps back nothing for himself.

—St. Jerome

804 The price of the kingdom is the food you give to those who need it.

—Pope St. Leo the Great

805 Never look a gift horse in the mouth.

—St. Jerome

806 If God loves a cheerful giver in fleshly wealth, how much more in spiritual wealth.

—St. Augustine

807 She preferred to store her money in the stomachs of the needy rather than hide it in a purse.

—St. Jerome

808 Do not hesitate to give, nor complain when you give.

—Pseudo-Barnabas

809 Hospitality is occupied in what is useful for strangers; and guests are strangers; and friends are guests; and brethren are friends.

—St. Clement of Alexandria

810 Every family should have a room where Christ is welcome in the person of the hungry and thirsty stranger.

—St. John Chrysostom

811 You do wrong to everyone you could help, but fail to help.

—St. Basil the Great

812 Let us not neglect Christ out of concern for our neighbor's illness, for we ought to love the sick for the sake of Christ.

—St. Augustine

813 Give Him the honor that He Himself asked for, by giving your money to the poor.

—St. John Chrysostom

814 Let us fill up what is lacking in our fasting with almsgiving for the poor.

—Pope St. Leo the Great

815 Let not those who need the aid of others be deserted by those they need.

—St. Augustine

816 Before all and above all, attention shall be paid to the sick, so that they shall be served as if they were Christ Himself.

—St. Benedict of Nursia

817 When it is in your power to do good, do not hold back, because alms deliver you from death.

—St. Polycarp of Smyrna

The World

818 The world was made and took its beginning at a certain time, and is to be destroyed on account of its wickedness.

—Origen

819 What the soul is to the body, so Christians are to the world.

—Anonymous (*Letter to Diognetus*)

820 Christians have no right to abandon their mission in the world, in the same way that the soul may not voluntarily separate itself from the body.

—Anonymous (*Letter to Diognetus*)

821 Nothing seemed to me so desirable as to close the doors of my senses and, escape from the flesh and the world — to recollect within myself, having no further connection than was absolutely necessary with human affairs — and to converse with myself and God, living superior to visible things, and ever preserving in myself the divine impressions pure and unmixed with the erring tokens of this lower world — to be, and to become constantly more and more, a real unspotted mirror of God and divine things, as light is added to light, till what was still dark grew clearer, enjoying already by hope the blessings of the world to come, roaming about with the angels, even now being above the earth by having forsaken it, and stationed on high by the Spirit.

—St. Gregory Nazianzen

822 They please the world most who please Christ least.

—St. Jerome

823 If it were better for the world not to exist, then why did God, in making the world, take the worse course? No, God did not work in vain or do what was worst. God ordered the creation with a view to its existence and continuance.

—St. Methodius of Olympus

Pleasure

824 The more one takes pleasure in lower things, the more he is separated from heavenly love.

—Pope St. Gregory the Great

825 Nothing that is simply pleasurable or merely sweet can please God. Everything must have in it a sharp seasoning of truth. Christ's passover must be eaten with bitter herbs.

—St. Jerome

826 What can be more pleasing than to scorn being pleased?

—Tertullian

827 Avoid wine as you would avoid poison. For wine is the first weapon used by demons against the young. . . . Wine and youth between them kindle the fire of sensual pleasure. Why throw oil on the flame — why add fresh fuel to a miserable body that is already ablaze?

—St. Jerome

828 Toward evening, about suppertime, when the serious studies of the day are over, is the time to take wine.

—St. Clement of Alexandria

829 The highest bodily pleasure, in the brightest earthly light, seemed unworthy of comparison to the sweetness of [eternal] life.

—St. Augustine

Community

830 We acknowledge one all-embracing common-wealth — the world.

—Tertullian

831 To ourselves, we seem many, but to God we are very few. We distinguish peoples and nations; to God, this whole world is one family.

—Minucius Felix

832 Man is the one name belonging to every nation on earth. There is one soul and many tongues, one spirit and many sounds. Every country has its own speech, but the subjects of speech are common to all.

—Tertullian

833 Our life and our death are with our neighbor. If we gain our brother, we have gained our God; but if we scandalize our brother, we have sinned against Christ.

—Anonymous (*Sayings of the Desert Fathers*)

834 We are the same to emperors as to our ordinary neighbors. For we are equally forbidden to wish ill, do ill, speak ill, think ill of all men.

—Tertullian

835 I am astonished when I think about the things men have studied to do for the hurt of their neighbors.

—St. Gregory the Wonderworker

836 Every guest . . . shall be received as if he were Christ Himself.

—St. Benedict of Nursia

Culture

837 I call him truly learned who brings everything to bear on the truth; so that, from geometry, music, grammar, and philosophy itself, culling what is useful, he guards the faith against assault.

—St. Clement of Alexandria

838 Whatever all men have uttered aright is the property of us Christians.

—St. Justin Martyr

839 Greek philosophy purifies the soul and prepares it to receive the faith on which truth constructs knowledge.

—St. Clement of Alexandria

840 Extract from Greek philosophy what may serve as a course of study or a preparation for Christianity, and from geometry and astronomy what will serve to explain the Sacred Scriptures, so that all that the sons of the philosophers say about geometry and music, grammar, rhetoric, and astronomy, as fellow-helpers to philosophy, we may say about philosophy itself in relation to Christianity.

—Origen

841 Greek culture, with its philosophy, came down from God to men, not with a definite direction, but in the way that showers fall on the good land, and on the dunghill, and on the houses.

—St. Clement of Alexandria

842 I embrace secular culture as a youthful handmaid; but Your knowledge I honor and reverence as true wife.

—St. Clement of Alexandria

843 Some, who think themselves naturally gifted, do not wish to touch either philosophy or logic; nor do they wish to learn natural science. They demand bare faith alone, as if they would, without giving any care to the vine, immediately gather clusters from the start.

—St. Clement of Alexandria

844 Each soul has its own proper food, some growing by knowledge and science, and others feeding on Greek philosophy, which in its entirety is, like nuts, not edible.

—St. Clement of Alexandria

845 What indeed has Athens to do with Jerusalem? What concord is there between the Academy and the Church? What between heretics and Christians? Our instruction comes from the Portico of Solomon (see Acts 3:11), who had himself taught that the Lord should be sought in simplicity of heart (see Wis 1:1).

—Tertullian

846 Childless indeed is pagan philosophy — always in pains of childbirth, it never engenders living offspring.

—St. Gregory of Nyssa

847 Nothing is more foreign to us Christians than politics.

—Tertullian

848 In the theatres, none of our senses is free from guilt, because our minds are tainted by evil desires, our ears by hearing, our eyes by seeing. Indeed, all the scenes are so disgraceful that a person cannot even describe them and talk about them without shame.

—Salvian

849 What shall I say of actors who make a public show of corruption? They teach men the tricks of adultery by performing them on the stage. By pretense, they train for reality.

—Lactantius

850 Actors are our instructors in infamy. Each spectator delights to see repeated on the stage what he has done at home, or hear what he may do on his return. Adultery is learned while it is seen.

—St. Cyprian

851 A certain woman went to the theatre and brought the devil home with her. In the exorcism, the unclean spirit was pressed and asked how he dared attack a Christian. "I have done nothing," he said, "but what I can justify, for I seized her upon my own ground."

—Tertullian

Evangelization

852 When you discover that something has been of benefit to you, you want to tell others about it. . . . Apply this human behavior to the spiritual realm: When you go to God, do not go alone.

— Pope St. Gregory the Great

853 Convert those who do not believe with the example of your life, so that your faith has a motive. If God's Word pleases you, act accordingly — not only God's Word in your heart, but in your life so that you will form God's family, united and pleasing to His eyes in all your actions. Don't doubt, brethren, that if your lives are worthy of God, unbelievers will find faith.

—St. Augustine

854 The eyes of all are turned upon you. Your house is set on a watchtower; your life fixes for others the limits of their self-control.

—St. Jerome

855 What do I desire? What do I want? Why do I speak? Why do I live, if not for this reason: that together we might live with Christ. . . . I do not want to be saved without you.

—St. Augustine

856 One loving heart sets another on fire.

—St. Augustine

857 The necessity of love seeks out the activity of the apostolate.

—St. Augustine

858 The fact that our number is increasing daily is no proof of error, but evidence of merit. For when men live an honorable life, their own friends remain constant and are joined by others.

—Minucius Felix

859 The throng of skin-clad savages who used to offer human sacrifices in honor of the dead have broken out of their harsh discord into the sweet music of the Cross, and Christ is the one cry of the whole world.

—St. Jerome

860 If we were truly Christian, there would not be a single pagan left.

—St. John Chrysostom

861 We who are without fear are not seeking to frighten you. But we would save all men if possible by warning them not to fight with God.

—Tertullian

862 As you move forward, attract others to go along with you. Desire to have companions on the road to the Lord.

—Pope St. Gregory the Great

863 Among your pearls count also the distinctive religious observances of your daily life. The more you try to conceal them, the more they arouse a pagan's curiosity.

—Tertullian

864 I was public enough in my profession of rhetoric. I ought not to be afraid of professing salvation.

—St. Augustine

865 The Church, shone over with the light of the Lord, sheds forth her rays over the whole world, yet it is one light that is everywhere diffused.

—St. Cyprian

866 Let not the Church possess wealth; let her possess souls, and if this is sufficient for her, let it be in marvelous measure!

—St. Ephrem of Syria

867 Save your soul in saving others.

—St. Jerome

Suffering

868 Let your afflictions be books to admonish you.
—St. Ephrem of Syria

869 God measures out affliction to our need.
—St. John Chrysostom

870 One and the same violence of affliction proves, purifies, and melts the good, and condemns, wastes, and casts out the bad.

—St. Augustine

871 The misfortune of evils does not kill you but instructs you. The suffering of adversity does not degrade you but exalts you. Human tribulation teaches you; it does not destroy you.

—St. Isidore of Seville

872 The house of mourning teaches charity and wisdom.
—St. John Chrysostom

873 Grief and death were born of sin, and devour sin.
—St. John Chrysostom

874 Sorrow is given to us on purpose, to cure us of sin.
—St. John Chrysostom

875 When we feel and suffer the human mischiefs of the body, that is not punishment — it is warfare.
—Minucius Felix

876 Fortitude is strengthened by infirmities, and calamity is very often the discipline of virtue.

—Minucius Felix

877 The earth, the vine, and the olive are in need of chastisement. When the olive is bruised, then its fruit smells sweet. When the vine is pruned, then its grapes are good. When the soil is plowed, its yield is good. When water is confined in channels, desert places drink of it; brass, silver, and gold, when they are burnished, shine.

—St. Ephrem of Syria

878 There is a joy that is affliction; misery is hidden within it. There is a misery that is profit; it is a fountain of joys in the new world.

—St. Ephrem of Syria

879 When matters come to extreme danger, and there is no longer any means of escape, how people flock together to the Church — of both sexes and all ages — begging for baptism, or reconciliation, or even for works of penance, each and all of them wanting consolation. consecration, and application of the sacraments.

—St. Augustine

880 They never remember God, unless they are in trouble.

—Lactantius

881 When men wish old age for themselves, what else do they wish but lengthened infirmity?

—St. Augustine

882 Ruin is like a loan shark. The greater the sum of dignity and office, the greater is the interest in penalties that a man has to pay.

—St. Cyprian of Carthage

883 I am, even now, a slave. But when I suffer, I shall be the freedman of Jesus, and shall rise again emancipated in Him.

—St. Ignatius of Antioch

884 If sorrow makes us shed tears, faith in God's promises makes us dry them.

—St. Augustine

885 Blessed is he who bears affliction with thankfulness.

—Anonymous (*Sayings of the Desert Fathers*)

Struggle

886 If you say "enough," you are lost. Go further, keep going. Don't stay in the same place, don't go back, don't go off the road.

—St. Augustine

887 What saint has ever won his crown without first contending for it?

—St. Jerome

888 A man becomes a Christian; he is not born one.

—Tertullian

889 Run, labor, sweat, fight against sadness. Hope comes with labor, and the palm is given to victory.

—Commodianus

890 My inability is as great as my desire.

—St. Basil the Great

891 God has desired that in spiritual combat we might fight rather with prayers than with our own strength.

—St. Augustine

892 We must love Christ and always seek His embraces. Then everything difficult will seem easy.

—St. Jerome

893 Never let suggestions of evil grow on you, or a babel of disorder win strength in your breast. Slay the enemy while he is small; and, that you may not have a crop of tares, nip the evil in the bud.

—St. Jerome

894 Time alone is the remedy of ills that time has matured.

—St. Basil the Great

895 Though remission of sins is given equally to all, the communion of the Holy Spirit is bestowed in proportion to each man's faith. If you have labored little, you receive little; but if you have worked much, the reward is great. You are running for yourself; see to your own interest.

—St. Cyril of Jerusalem

896 Spread your sails, fasten the Cross as an ensign on your prow. The calm that you speak of is itself a tempest.

—St. Jerome

897 Why are there so many snares? That we may not fly low, but seek the things that are above.

—St. John Chrysostom

898 Show in ascetic exercise that your heart is strengthened. Cleanse your vessel, that you may receive grace more abundantly.

—St. Cyril of Jerusalem

899 All of us who enter the arena of the faith are committed to fight against evil spirits.

—Pope St. Gregory the Great

900 Demons injure only those who fear them, whom the powerful and lofty hand of God does not protect, who are uninitiated in the mystery of truth. But they fear the righteous, the worshipers of God.

—Lactantius

901 Let us charge into the good fight with joy and love without being afraid of our enemies. Though unseen themselves, they can look at the face of our soul, and if they see it altered by fear, they take up arms against us all the more fiercely. For the cunning creatures have observed that we are scared. So let us take up arms against them courageously. No one will fight with a resolute fighter.

—St. John of the Ladder

902 When an archer wants to shoot his arrows successfully, he first takes great pains over his posture and lines himself up accurately with his mark. It should be the same for you who are about to shoot the head of the wicked devil. Let us be concerned first for the good order of sensations and then for the good posture of inner thoughts.

—St. John Chrysostom

903 Living this life, let us be carefully on our guard and, as is written, "with all watchfulness, keep our heart" (Prv 4:23). For we have enemies, powerful and crafty — the wicked demons; and it is against these that we wrestle.

—St. Anthony of Egypt

904 Evil spirits, since they can do nothing, are but as actors in a play, changing their shapes and frightening children by their tumult and their make-believe.

—St. Anthony of Egypt

905 Ask, on my behalf, both inward and outward strength, that I may not only speak, but truly will; and that I may not merely be *called* a Christian, but may really prove to be one. For if I prove myself a Christian, I may also be called one, and then be deemed faithful.

—St. Ignatius of Antioch

906 Do not be surprised that you fall every day; do not give up, but stand your ground courageously. And surely the angel who guards you will honor your patience.

—St. John of the Ladder

907 As much as you watch over your mind carelessly, by so much will you become distant from Jesus.

—Hesychius of Jerusalem

908 The reward of self-control is interior freedom.

—St. Maximus the Confessor

909 I was amazed by their perseverance in prayer, and at their triumphing over sleep. Subdued by no natural necessity, they ever kept their souls' purpose high and free, in hunger, thirst, cold, nakedness, never yielding to the body. They were never willing to waste attention on it. As if living in a flesh that was not theirs, they showed in very deed what it means to sojourn for a while in this life, and what it means to have one's citizenship and home in heaven.

—St. Basil the Great

910 Blot out from your mind all earthly care, for you are running for your soul. You are utterly forsaking the things of the world. Small are the things you are forsaking; great what the Lord is giving. Forsake things present, and put your trust in things to come.

—St. Cyril of Jerusalem

911 Let me be an imitator of the passion of my God.
—St. Ignatius of Antioch

912 What toil we must endure, what fatigue, while we are attempting to climb hills and the summits of mountains! What, that we may ascend to heaven! If you consider the promised reward, what you endure is less. Immortality is given to the one who perseveres; everlasting life is offered; the Lord promises His kingdom.
—St. Cyprian of Carthage

913 The madness of anger should be controlled; the downcast look of dejection overcome; vain glory should be despised, the disdainfulness of pride trampled under foot, and the shifting and wandering thoughts of the mind restrained by continual recollection of God. And the slippery wanderings of our heart should be brought back again to the contemplation of God as often as our crafty enemy, in his attempts to lead away the mind a captive from this consideration, creeps into the innermost recesses of the heart.
—St. John Cassian

914 Order your soul. Reduce your wants. Live in charity. Associate in Christian community. Obey the laws. Trust in providence.
—St. Augustine

915 You are about to pass through a noble struggle, in which the living God acts the part of umpire, in which the Holy Spirit is your trainer, in which the prize is an eternal crown of angelic essence, citizenship in the heavens, glory everlasting.
—Tertullian

916 Christians always — and now more than ever — pass their times not in gold but in iron.

—Tertullian

917 Most miserable, ever sick with the fevers of impatience, I need to sigh after and invoke and persistently plead for that healthy patience which I do not have.

—Tertullian

918 It is impossible for a full belly to make trial of the combat of the inner man: nor is he worthy to be tried in harder battles, who can be overcome in a slight skirmish.

—St. John Cassian

919 The athlete of Christ — after gaining victory over the rebellious flesh, after casting it as it were under his feet — is carried forward as triumphing on high.

—St. John Cassian

920 The athlete of Christ, as long as he is in the body, is never in want of a victory to be gained in contests: but in proportion as he grows by triumphant successes, so does a more severe kind of struggle confront him.

—St. John Cassian

921 If a man is unable to check the unnecessary desires of the appetite, how will he be able to extinguish the fire of carnal lust?

—St. John Cassian

922 Our foe is shut up within ourselves; an internal warfare is daily waged by us. And if we are victorious, all external things will be made weak, and everything will be made peaceful and subdued for the soldier of Christ.

—St. John Cassian

923 We shall have no external enemy to fear, if what is within is overcome and subdued to the spirit.

—St. John Cassian

924 All lust and shifty wanderings of heart are a sort of food for the soul, nourishing it on harmful meats, but leaving it afterwards without share of the heavenly bread and of really solid food.

—St. John Cassian

925 If, while fasting in the body, we are entangled in the most dangerous vices of the soul, our humiliation of the flesh will do us no good whatever

—St. John Cassian

926 Do not entangle yourself in the affairs of this life, for you are fighting for God.

—St. Ambrose

927 Live every day as if dying.

—St. Anthony of Egypt

928 The beginning has been well ordered. Now may I win grace to cling to my lot without hindrance to the end.

—St. Ignatius of Antioch

Persecution

929 It becomes a Christian to die in ashes. If I set any other example, I should sin myself.

—St. Martin of Tours

930 Come fire and the cross! Come the crowds of wild beasts! Come tearings, breakings, and dislocations of bones! Come cutting off of members; come shatterings of the whole body! Let all the dreadful torments of the devil come upon me! Only let me attain to Jesus Christ.

—St. Ignatius of Antioch

931 Though beheaded, and crucified, and thrown to wild beasts, in chains and fire, and all other tortures, we do not give up our confession; but the more such things happen, the more others, in larger numbers, become believers.

—St. Justin Martyr

932 The more often you mow us down, the more in number we grow. The blood of Christians is seed.

—Tertullian

933 I am the wheat of God. Let me be ground by the teeth of the wild beasts, that I may be found the pure bread of Christ.

—St. Ignatius of Antioch

934 I give You thanks that You have counted me worthy of this day and this hour, that I should have a part in the number of Your martyrs . . . among whom may I be accepted this day before You as a rich and acceptable sacrifice, as You, the ever-truthful God, have foreordained.

—St. Polycarp of Smyrna

935 What do bright and spacious mansions have to compare in value with that murky, filthy, smelly, and tormenting prison undergone for God's sake?

—St. John Chrysostom

936 How can you be excused if — at a time when others are persecuted, exiled, and otherwise harassed — you do not exert yourself for your distressed people, either by your presence or by your teaching?

—St. John Chrysostom

937 Persecution does not diminish but increases the Church, and the Lord's field is clothed with an ever richer crop, while the grains, which fall singly, spring up and are multiplied a hundredfold.

—Pope St. Leo the Great

938 Each soul that has lived purely in the knowledge of God, and has obeyed the commandments, is a martyr both by life and word, no matter how it may be released from the body — shedding faith as blood along its whole life, till its departure.

—St. Clement of Alexandria

939 When the persecution finally ceased . . . he left and went back to his solitary cell; and there he was a daily martyr to his conscience, ever fighting the battles of the faith. For he practiced a zealous and more intense ascetic life.

—St. Athanasius

940 This community will be undying. For, be assured, that just in the time of its seeming overthrow it is built up into greater power. For all who witness the noble patience of its martyrs are inflamed with desire to examine into the matter in question. And as soon as they come to know the truth, they immediately enroll themselves as disciples.

—Tertullian

941 In time of persecution it is better to flee from place to place, as we are permitted, than to be arrested and to deny the faith under torture.

—Tertullian

942 [Martyrdom] is a baptism greater in grace, more sublime in power, more precious in honor, a baptism that the angels administer.

—St. Cyprian of Carthage

943 How many people are hidden martyrs for Christ each day, confessing the Lord Jesus with their deeds!

—St. Ambrose of Milan

944 May those who persecute us believe and live, and in time rejoice with us in eternity.

—St. Cyprian of Carthage

Death

945 Every day we are changing, every day we are dying, and yet we fancy ourselves eternal.

—St. Jerome

946 Apart from the knowledge of God, what solid happiness can there be, since death must come? Like a dream, happiness slips away before it is grasped.

—Minucius Felix

947 What is death at most? It is a journey for a season; a sleep longer than usual. If you fear death, you should also fear sleep.

—St. John Chrysostom

948 The body in the tomb is like the trees that hide their green in winter with a deceptive dryness. Why are you impatient for it to revive and return while the winter is still raw? We, too, must wait for the springtime of the body.

—Minucius Felix

949 What is dying? Just the same as putting off a garment. For the body is about the soul as a garment, and after laying this aside for a short time by means of death, we shall take it up again with more splendor.

—St. John Chrysostom

950 They are in error who either desire death as a good or flee from life as an evil.

—Lactantius

951 The upright, righteous, good, and wise neither fear nor tremble at death, because of the great hope that is before them. And at all times they are mindful of death, their exodus, and of the last day, when the children of Adam shall be judged.

—St. Aphrahat

952 People are unable to thread the turns of mazes until they happen to fall in with someone who has experience of them. Then, by following behind, they get to the end of those various misleading turns in the chambers. This they could not do, if they did not follow their leader step by step. So, too, the labyrinth of our life cannot be threaded by the faculties of human nature unless one pursues that same path as He, Who entered it once, yet got beyond the difficulties which hemmed Him in. I apply this figure of a labyrinth to that prison of death, which is without an egress and surrounds the wretched race of mankind.

—St. Gregory of Nyssa

Hell

953 Death is the dissolution of the nature of living beings; death is the separation of body and soul. But this is how we define the second death: Death is the suffering of eternal pain; death is the condemnation of souls to the eternal punishments that they deserve.

—Lactantius

954 The perpetual death of the damned will go on without end and will be their common lot, regardless of what people, prompted by human sentiments, may conjure up.

—St. Augustine

955 There is no room for rashness here. If we are deceived either by empty character or false opinion, we must endure the punishment of our folly for all eternity.

—Lactantius

956 Hell is paved with the skulls of priests.

—St. John Chrysostom

957 He fashioned hell for the inquisitive.

—St. Augustine

Saints

958 A man should not be mourned if, after conquering and triumphing over the world, he has at last received the crown of justice.

—Sulpicius

959 Christianity is not only a thing of silence, but also of manifest greatness.

—St. Ignatius of Antioch

960 The saints are like a group of trees, each bearing different fruit, but watered from the same source. The practices of one saint differ from those of another, but it is the same Spirit that works in all of them.

—Anonymous (*Sayings of the Desert Fathers*)

961 The imitation of those who have already been proved, and who have led correct lives, is most excellent for the understanding and practice of the commandments.

—St. Clement of Alexandria

962 Let us carefully review the life of [the saints], and let us emulate their faith and love and hope and zeal and way of life, and endurance of sufferings and patience even to blood, in order that we may be sharers with them in their crowns of glory.

—St. John of Damascus

963 You are not a perfect ascetic if you have the food, drink, and bed of St. John the Baptist. In order to reach perfection, you must have his spirit.

—St. Isidore of Pelusium

964 It is not right to glory in casting out devils, nor in curing diseases, nor to make much of him who casts out devils and to undervalue him who does not. Instead, study the ascetic life of this man and that, and either imitate and emulate or improve it. For to do miracles is not ours, but the Savior's.

—St. Anthony of Egypt

965 The first saints were shepherds.

—St. Augustine

966 The saints must be honored as friends of Christ and sons and heirs of God.

—St. John of Damascus

967 In psalms and hymns and spiritual songs, in contrition and in pity for the needy, let us believers honor the saints, as God too is much honored in this way.

—St. John of Damascus

968 Let us raise monuments to [the saints] and visible images, and let us ourselves become, through imitation of their virtues, living monuments and images of them.

—St. John of Damascus

969 In the relics of the saints the Lord Christ has provided us with saving fountains, which in many ways pour out gifts and gush with fragrant ointments.

—St. John of Damascus

970 Blessed be God, who selects those in each generation who are pleasing to Him and makes known the vessels of His election, and uses them for the ministry of the saints.

—St. Basil the Great

Angels

971 Every angel and demon is winged. Thus they are everywhere in a moment. To them the whole world is one place.

—Tertullian

972 Beauty is not necessary to God's angels.

—Tertullian

973 We should pray to the angels, for they are given to us as guardians.

—St. Ambrose of Milan

974 We recognize a multitude of angels and ministers whom God the Maker and Framer of the world distributed and posted to their various posts by the Word, to occupy themselves about the elements, the heavens, the world and the things in it, and the goodly ordering of them all.

—Athenagoras of Athens

975 The angels must be petitioned for us, who have been given to us to guard us.

—St. Ambrose of Milan

Mary

976 No one may understand the meaning of the Gospel if he has not rested on the breast of Jesus and received Mary from Jesus, to be his mother also.

—Origen

977 The Lord selected his mother from the posterity of Abraham and assumed flesh from her. Thus He was in truth made man, in all like us, except sin.

—St. Isidore of Pelusium

978 Christ chose for Himself the special gift of virginity, and showed forth the privilege of integrity, representing, as He did, in Himself what He had chosen for His mother.

—St. Ambrose of Milan

979 A correct, sufficient, and irreproachable profession of faith is found in the assertion of the divine maternity of the Blessed Virgin.

—Cyril of Alexandria

980 If anyone does not believe that Holy Mary is the Mother of God, he is severed from the Godhead.

—St. Gregory Nazianzen

981 Death came through Eve; life has come through Mary.

—St. Jerome

982 We proclaim the holy Virgin to be properly and truly Mother of God. For, as He Who was born of her is true God, so is she truly Mother of God who gave birth to the true God Who took His flesh from her.

—St. John of Damascus

983 What the womb of Mary did with the flesh of Christ, let your heart do with the law of Christ.

—St. Augustine

984 Mary symbolizes the Church, which, espoused to Christ as a virgin, has conceived us of the Holy Spirit, and as a virgin has also given us birth.

—St. Isidore of Seville

985 The prayers of His mother are a pleasure to the Son, because He desires to grant all that is granted on her account, and thus repay her for the favor she gave Him in giving His body.

—St. Theophilus of Alexandria

986 Blessed are you. You are a second heaven upon earth.

—Anonymous (Ethiopian hymn)

987 O holy Mother of God, remember us who boast of you, and who in noble hymns celebrate the memory that will ever live and never fade away.

—St. Methodius of Olympus

988 Hail to you forever, O virgin mother of God, our unceasing joy. . . . You are the pearl of great price that belongs to the kingdom; the fate of every victim, the living altar of the bread of life. Hail, O treasure of the love of God. Hail, O fount of the Son's love for man.

—St. Methodius of Olympus

989 "Behold, I am the handmaid of the Lord; let it be to me according to your word" (Lk 1:38). . . . Thus was the knot of Eve's disobedience loosed by the obedience of Mary. . . . As the human race fell into bondage to death by means of a virgin, so it is rescued by a virgin. Virginal disobedience was balanced in the opposite scale by virginal obedience. In the same way, the sin of the first created man receives amendment by the First-begotten, and the coming of the serpent is conquered by the harmlessness of the dove, unloosing those chains that had bound us to death.

—St. Irenaeus of Lyons

990 Truly tremendous is the mystery connected with you, O virgin mother, spiritual throne, glorified and made worthy of God! You have brought forth, before the eyes of those in heaven and earth, a preeminent wonder. . . . Blessed are you among the generations of women, O you most blessed by God, for by you the earth has been filled with that divine glory of God.

—St. Methodius of Olympus

991 What a day will that be when Mary, the Lord's mother, shall come to meet you, attended with virgin choirs.

—St. Jerome

Glory

992 Join yourself to the eternal God and you shall be eternal.

—St. Augustine

993 We know full well that, of all things fair and honorable, the best is to possess God forever.

—St. Gregory Nazianzen

994 Hail, O light! For in us, buried in darkness, shut up in the shadow of death, light has shone forth from heaven, purer than the sun, sweeter than life here below. That light is eternal life.

—St. Clement of Alexandria

995 The sage and Christian both must die; but the one always dies out of his glory, the other into it.

—St. Jerome

996 My love has been crucified, and there is no fire within me desiring to be fed; but there is within me a water that lives and speaks, saying to me inwardly, "Come to the Father." I have no delight in perishable food, nor in the pleasures of this life. I desire the bread of God, the heavenly bread, the bread of life, which is the flesh of Jesus Christ, the Son of God, from the seed of David and Abraham; and I desire the drink of God, namely His blood, which is incorruptible love and eternal life.

—St. Ignatius of Antioch

997 At the resurrection, the substance of our bodies, however disintegrated, will be reunited. We must not fear that the omnipotence of God cannot recall all the particles that have been consumed by fire or by beasts, or dissolved into dust and ashes, or decomposed into water, or evaporated into air.

—St. Augustine

998 Then the rain of blessing shall descend from God at morning and evening, and the earth shall bring forth all her fruit without the labor of men. Honey shall drop from rocks, fountains of milk and wine shall abound. The beasts shall lay aside their ferocity and become mild, the wolf shall roam among the flocks without doing harm, the calf shall feed with the lion, the dove shall be united with the hawk, the serpent shall have no poison; no animal shall live by bloodshed. For God shall supply to all abundant and harmless food.

—Lactantius

999 Though men should say much, they shall not be able to express it. . . . Yet it is right for a speaker to compare and call that place "the abode of God," and "the place of life," "the perfect place," "the place of light," "the place of glory," "the Sabbath of God," "the day of rest," "the repose of the righteous," "the joy of the just," "the abode and dwelling-place of the righteous and the holy," "the place of our hope," "the sure abode of our trust," "the place of our treasure," "the place that shall assuage our weariness and remove our afflictions, and soothe our sighs."

—St. Aphrahat

1000 Let us not cheat ourselves of all this power, glory, blessedness by bartering the enjoyment of all eternal things for a brief season of pleasure that cannot last.

—Nemesius of Emesa

Ancient Writers Quoted in This Book

Dates are approximate.

St. Alexander of Alexandria (d. 328)
St. Ambrose of Milan (d. 397)
St. Aphrahat (d. 345)
St. Archelaus (d. 282)
St. Aristides (second century)
Arnobius (d. 330)
St. Athanasius (d. 373)
Athenagoras (second century)
St. Augustine of Hippo (d. 430)
St. Basil the Great (d. 379)
St. Benedict of Nursia (d. 550)
St. Callistus, Pope (d. 222)
Cassiodorus (d. 580)
St. Clement of Alexandria (d. 215)
St. Clement I of Rome, Pope (reigned 88-97)
Commodianus (third century?)
St. Cyprian of Carthage (d. 258)
St. Cyril of Alexandria (d. 444)
St. Cyril of Jerusalem (d. 386)
Diodicus (fifth century)
St. Dionysius the Great (d. 264)
Didymus the Blind (d. 398)
St. Epiphanius (d. 403)
St. Ephrem of Syria (d. 373)
Eusebius of Caesarea (d. 340)
St. Gregory of Nazianzus (d. 390)

St. Gregory of Nyssa (d. 395)
St. Gregory I the Great, Pope (reigned 590-604)
St. Gregory the Wonderworker (d. 270)
Hesychius of Jerusalem (d. 433)
St. Hippolytus of Rome (d. 236)
St. Ignatius of Antioch (d. 107)
St. Irenaeus of Lyons (d. 202)
St. Isidore of Pelusium (d. 450)
St. Isidore of Seville (d. 636)
St. Jerome (d. 420)
St. John Cassian (d. 435)
St. John Chrysostom (d. 407)
St. John of the Ladder (d. 649)
St. John of Damascus (d. 749)
St. Justin Martyr (d. 165)
Lactantius (d. 323)
St. Leo I the Great, Pope (reigned 440-461)
St. Macarius (d. 390)
St. Martin of Tours (d. 397)
St. Maximus the Confessor (d. 662)
St. Melito of Sardis (d. 180)
St. Methodius of Olympus (d. 311)
Minucius Felix (second century)
Nemesius of Emesa (fourth century)
Origen (d. 254)
St. Polycarp of Smyrna (d. 155)
Pseudo-Barnabas (first century)
Pseudo-Clement (second century)
Pseudo-Dionysius the Areopagite (sixth century)
Salvian (fifth century)
Synesius of Cyrene (d. 414)
Tertullian (d. 222)
Theodoret of Cyrrhus (d. 458)
St. Theophilus of Antioch (second century)
St. Vincent of Lerins (d. 450)

Also by Mike Aquilina

With David Scott. Selected readings from Dorothy Day's spiritual director Father J. Hugo.

0-87973-**920**-7, paper, $14.95, 336 pp.

With Fr. Kris D. Stubna. The best-selling book on the basic truths and teachings of the Catholic Church in question-and-answer format.

0-87973-**574**-0, paper, $5.95, 112 pp.

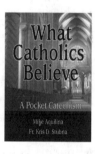

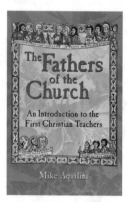

Biographies of 25 of the leading Fathers of the Church, including Clement, Justin Martyr, Ambrose, Jerome, and Augustine.

0-97973-**689**-5, paper, $10.95, 240 pp.

From Our Sunday Visitor 1-800-348-2440
or http://www.osv.com